The
POWER of
LEADERSHIP
METAPHORS

200 prompts to stimulate
your imagination & creativity

PETER SHAW

Marshall Cavendish
Business

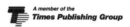

Dedicated to our grandchildren,
Barney, Daniel, Ruth, Jacob, Lucca, Lucas and Stellan
with thanks for all the joy they give us.

CONTENTS

21. A picture is worth a thousand words
22. Don't kill the goose that lays the golden egg
23. Look beyond the end of your nose
24. The immediate can drive out the important

Section B: Values

25 Hope springs eternal
26 A close shave
27 Life is a roundabout
28 The dog that didn't bark
29 Keep watch
30 Know when to keep your distance
31 The elephant in the room
32 Bury the hatchet
33 Draw the line
34 Face the music
35 Don't waste a crisis
36 People in glass house should not throw stones
37 We have two ears and one mouth
38 None so deaf as those who will not hear
39 Connect brain to mouth
40 No smoke without fire
41 Once bitten twice shy
42 Silence gives consent
43 Don't feel you have to fill the silence
44 The least said the soonest mended
45 Truth will out
46 Truth has many dimensions
47. Watch getting steamed up
48. Be mindful if you are giving the cold shoulder
49. Actions speak louder than words
50. All that glitters is not gold

51. As you sow so shall you reap
52. Watch if familiarity breeds contempt
53. You can't make a silk purse out of a sow's ear

Section C: Value-added

54. A foot in the door
55. The first rocks in the jar
56. Build on rock and not on sand
57 The hoop you have to jump through
58. Three steps forward and two steps back
59. Go slow to go fast
60. Be careful what you wish for
61. Steering not rowing
62. Armed to the teeth
63. Lion-hearted
64. Wait till the clouds roll by
65. Soaring and swooping like an eagle
66. Keep your powder dry
67. Nip in the bud
68. The early bird catches the worm
69 Strike while the iron is hot
70 Keep the pot boiling
71. Take the bull by the horns
72. A cat may look at a king
73. Make hay while the sun shines
74. Know the ropes
75. Half a loaf is better than none
76. Fortune knocks once on every door
77. Two heads are better than one
78. Too many cooks spoil the broth
79. A stitch in time saves nine
80. Be alert to the domino effect

81. Put your best foot forward
82. Seek to ensure both ends meet
83. Among the blind the one-eyed man is king
84. Better late than never
85. Discretion is the better part of valour
86. Be on the balcony and on the dance floor
87. Use the long screwdriver occasionally
88. A germ of truth
89. Conversations in the grey space
90. Three strikes and you are out
91. Be ready for the wake-up call

Section D: Vitality

92. Put a tiger in your tank
93. Don't hit your head against a brick wall
94. A walk in the park
95. Walk before you run
96. Take deep breaths
97. What goes up comes down
98. Show a clean pair of heals
99. Hold your tongue
100. Chew the fat
101. Turn over a new leaf
102. Go on all fours
103. Take forty winks
104. Still small voice of calm
105. Absence makes the heart grow fonder
106. Any time means no time
107. Leave well alone
108. He laughs best who laughs last
109. A penny saved is a penny gained
110. No pain no gain

111. Still waters run deep
112. Beware going into overdrive
113. Watch the chip on the shoulder
114. Watch if your heart is in your boots
115. Keep your distance
116. A cat has nine lives
117. An idle brain is the Devil's workshop
118. An ounce of protection is worth a pound of cure
119. A task begun is half done
120. Beauty is only skin deep
121. Better to wear out than rust out
122. Cross the stream where it is at its shallowest
123. Laugh and the world laughs with you
124. Bottle the positives

Section E: Risks to watch: beware lest you
125. Turn up your nose
126. Live from hand to mouth
127. Act the goat
128. Ride the high horse
129. Play with fire
130. Let the cat out of the bag
131. Rush from pillar to post
132. Create a storm in a teacup
122. Are the fly in the ointment
134. Clutch at straws
135. Are left high and dry
136. Nurture a pet lamb who becomes a cross ram
137. Grasp all and lose all
138. Run into a brick wall
139. Flog a dead horse
140. Slide down a slippery slope

141. Be alert to when you have cold feet
142. Expect everything to be copper bottomed
143. Are a wet blanket
144. Get carried away with excitement
145. Are viewed as being as blind as a bat
146. Are seen as a peppery individual
147. Are always sat on the fence
148. Are seen as playing fast and loose
149. Get into hot water
150. Throw in the sponge too early
151. Put the cart before the horse
152. Are burning the candle at both ends
153. Jump the gun
154. Are always throwing cold water
155. Are seen as blind to behaviours
156. Are seen as a flash in a pan
157. Bite the hand that feeds
158. Count your chickens before they hatch
159. Judge a book by its cover
160. Disappear without trace
161. Be captive to your former self
162. Jump in where angels fear to tread
163. Shoot the messenger
164. Be a slave to ambition

Section F: Lessons from Shakespeare

165. Delays have dangerous ends
166. Blown with the windy tempest of my heart
167. My salad days when I was green in judgement
168. From hour to hour we ripe and ripe. And then from hour to hour we rot and rot
169. Brevity is the soul of wit

170. By indirections find directions out
171. The wheel has come full circle
172. There is no virtue like necessity
173. More in sorrow than anger
174. Hoist with his own petard

Section G: Our attitude of mind
175. Let a thousand flowers bloom
176. The road not taken
177. See life as a marathon and not a sprint
178. Take the lid off
179. Look through the other end of the telescope
180. Watch getting caught in the vortex
181. Watch dwelling on broken dreams
182. Beware getting caught in a huddle of anger
183. The blame-game is easy and self-destructive
184. The puzzled shrug of the shoulders

Section H: Eternal truths
185. As you make your bed you must lie on it
186. Cut your coat according to your cloth
187. Withdraw gracefully
188. Don't carry all your eggs in one basket
189. Every cloud has a silver lining
190. Experience teaches fools
191. Pride comes before a fall
192. Turkeys don't vote for Christmas
193. Remove the beam from your eye first
194. Fire is a good servant and a bad master
195. He who pays the piper calls the tune
196. It's a long lane with no turning
197. Sauce for goose is sauce for the gander

Foreword

As a leader you have to create a context for dialogue. You need to know where you are going and what it is realistic to achieve, but you also have to create the environment where people want to travel with you.

You need to put in place a structure which encourages people to tell you what they think, to tell you when you are wrong and be willing to engage with you to find a workable way forward. You need to keep listening to concerns that are spoken and unspoken; far too many leaders listen to those who tell them what they want to hear and forget the lesson of "the Emperor's new clothes". You also have to decide which battles to fight and when to stand back and let issues play out. Key is deciding which issues you want to pursue and then to communicate clearly the reasons for your decisions.

There are times as a leader when you are patiently waiting for opportunities. On other occasions you know you need to intervene in order to steer, shape or nudge a way forward. At times the decision-making and resources are in the hands of others, but you must, when appropriate, use your voice and influence. You are ready to make a suggestion or express a concern when the right moment arises.

When I was Lord Chief Justice with responsibility for the Judiciary in England and Wales the Judges looked to me to take a lead and set a tone. I engaged with a wide range of different interests including the City and business, Government ministers, civil servants, the legal professions, public interest groups, the media and judges throughout the world. They all brought particular concerns and were looking to me to work together within our respective responsibilities to find pragmatic ways forward.

Metaphors were a very powerful tool for me. Examples I particularly recall are the themes behind "time to blaze a trail" and "faint hearts never won fair lady". They were particularly apt in dealing with modernising the court system and taking advantage of the digital revolution; and, in a very different context, in getting the judiciaries of different nations to work together and support each other. But it is always necessary to have in mind each of the metaphors collected under the heading of "Eternal Truths" – they can save you from many a mistake.

Metaphors encapsulate the wisdom of collective experience in a few words. A metaphor which captures the visual imagination of an individual or group can help move a conversation forward in a creative way. This book provides an eclectic set of metaphors. Some are new and others are well known. Each of them is worth a few moments thought. Many will apply to leaders in a range of different contexts. I encourage you to let your imagination take forward the metaphors and then to reflect on the questions at the end of each section.

I have known Peter Shaw for over fifteen years during which we have had many stimulating conversations about leadership. More importantly he gave the judiciary very considerable assistance in developing leadership skills in discharging the judiciaries' new responsibilities, as he has done in other countries He brings a wealth of experience from his time as a Director General in the UK Civil Service and then working with a wide range of leaders and leadership teams across six continents as an executive coach and University Professor.

I commend this book highly as a source of rich prompting for leaders thinking through how best they steer and influence in a wide range of different situations.

Lord John Thomas
Lord Chief Justice of England and Wales 2013-2017
President of the Qatar International Court

Introduction

A story or picture is worth a thousand words. A story, picture or metaphor can help us crystallise what we need to do next. A phrase such as 'the seed has to die' or 'the light at the end of the tunnel' or 'the risk of not seeing the wood for the trees' can sum up in a poignant way truths that we as leaders need to recognise.

As we explore a metaphor next steps can become clearer. A metaphor can stimulate our imagination and allow us to think afresh about an issue. Reflecting on a problem using a metaphor can help us unblock our thinking and open up the possibility of new solutions. It can enable us to 'cut to the heart of an issue', clarify situations, provide insights or show us where we are stuck. They can enable us to face into the reality that we need to abandon a project, make a fresh start or change direction.

I often use metaphors in coaching conversations and find they lead to creative and stimulating dialogue. Some are well know metaphors and others are ones I have picked up from a myriad of sources, and some either I or someone I work with has devised. Sometimes in the midst of a coaching conversation a phrase comes to mind that encapsulates an idea or way forward. The metaphor that is memorable allows an idea to stick in the memory and be a constant reminder that there is a way forward which may be different to what we had previously anticipated.

I include in this book 200 metaphors that ring true for me. I am using the word metaphor loosely as some of the phrases included in the book might be described as proverbs, idioms or aphorisms. Writing one on each page allows the reader to absorb quickly the applicability of the metaphor and then to reflect at leisure on its relevance for them. I prompt the reader through a paragraph about each metaphor followed by a short illustration of its relevance to a leader and then three prompts or questions for reflection. Within each section the short illustrations relate to a hypothetical leader whose experiences draw from my own observations in both leadership roles and coaching conversations. These hypothetical individuals are Ben, Gillian, William, Saira, Harry, Carol, Brenda and Rashid.

The underlying approach I use in coaching is to encourage people to reflect on the four Vs of leadership: namely vision, values, value-add and vitality. This was the framework I originally set out in the book of this title published by Capstone in 2006. A Praesta Insight with this title was published in 2019 which set out the continuing relevance of this approach for individuals and teams and included perspectives from leaders who have found the framework helpful.

The first part of this book groups the metaphors under the themes of vision, values, value-add and vitality. A subsequent section includes metaphors about risks to watch. Ten poignant metaphors written by Shakespeare provide evocative reminders, although there are many more that there was not space to include such as 'all the world's a stage and all men and women merely players: they have their exits and their entrances.' The final section identifies other metaphors as eternal truths.

As a result of the Covid 19 pandemic we are living in a very different world with profound economic and social changes where we need to think in new ways about leading and engaging. Some metaphors like 'bottling the positives' have been poignant over the pandemic period. The use of metaphors can be a useful way of opening up ways of addressing future unprecedented challenges.

The book is intended as a prompt for thought. My hope is that in every situation there will be a metaphor that holds your imagination and enables you to see an issue from a different perspective. Allow your imagination to play with each metaphor and open up the possibility of a new insight or possibility. Perhaps out of the darkest moments there can be new possibilities which might surprise and enthuse you.

Peter Shaw
Godalming, England

SECTION A

Vision

1
The seed has to die

An idea or belief has to die before new life and hope can break out.

You have kept up your resolve by being frustrated with the world around you. Your belief in your abilities has helped you be successful up to a point, but you begin to recognise that life cannot go on in quite in the same way. You need to calm down and let your belief that you are right diminish. You begin to recognise that you need to accept that new life and hope can break out when you allow others to flourish and allow your desire to prove yourself right diminish.

Ben was a skilled project manager who had built his reputation by being a good judge of what was needed in any situation. Ben began to recognise that others were deferring to him too much and were not making the decisions that they were capable of making. He needed to stand back more and not seek the limelight. He needed to ensure that others were in the lead so that they became increasingly enthused and positive about the future.

Reflections
- What self-belief or preoccupation needs to die so you can move on?
- What frustrations need to be diminished so they don't cloud your judgment?
- How best to you leave behind an outdated preoccupation?

2
When one door closes another opens

When one route forward is closed off you might see possibilities that had not been visible to you before.

You are keen to push forward and seek wider responsibilities. You observe an opportunity and want to see if it is an opening that you can take forward. As you ask questions or offer to help you begin to recognise that the opening is not for you as you don't match what is needed. You are disappointed and realistic at the same time. You begin to look at what else might be possible future options. When you thought through the initial possibility you clarified some of your ideas on what you can contribute. Other possibilities begin to shape in your mind.

Ben had explored moving to another project which did not happen. The application process had helped him crystallise his strengths. When the vacancy arose to lead the current project he was far better equipped to apply for it. Going for the job that did not materialise had shaped the way he now led his current team.

Reflections
* When do you stop pushing on a door that is not opening?
* How do you look out for new doors that might be opening?
* When you look back how grateful are you that some doors were firmly closed in your face?

3
The light at the end of the tunnel

When you allow yourself to peer forward there can be a glimpse of light far in the distance.

You are engrossed in an immediate issue. You feel stuck and are wary of looking too far ahead as this could mean you become depressed by the gloomy prospect of continuing darkness. It feels relentless with no possibility of better times ahead. You tell yourself that you have been in this type of situation before and the darkness has abated. Imagining what the light will be like when you reach it gives you hope that darkness can gradually diminish.

Ben was leading a project that was moving slowly. No one was delivering in the way expected. He had to be relentless in reminding participants of their commitments. Eventually there was unanimity about next steps and Ben allowed himself to believe that there was progress. When he peered into the future, he could glimpse the prospect of light at the end of this seemingly very dark tunnel.

Reflections
- What has helped you on previous occasions recognise that there will be light at the end of the tunnel?
- How best do you visualise light at the end of the tunnel without deluding yourself about the current issues?
- How might you describe to others what light at the end of the tunnel might look like?

4
The rocks in the way

The landscape needs to be surveyed carefully to assess what are the rocks in the way and how might they be overcome.

We see huge boulders ahead that are going to be difficult to climb. We don't feel equipped. How can we possibly get round them or over them? We know that we need to assess what is the shape of the rocks in the way. Are they scalable? Have we colleagues who have experience in dealing with such rocks? Are they more manageable than we had initially thought? What might be the routes around the rocks? Which rocks do we need to climb and which ones can we circumvent?

Ben saw one overriding issue as a big rock in the way. It seemed a problem that was going to be hugely difficult to resolve. He decided to look at the issue from different angles and draw in the view of people with different perspectives. A hugely daunting problem gradually became a difficult but manageable project. The rock blocking the way became an obstacle which could be overcome.

Reflections
- Who can help you see the rock from a different perspective?
- What expertise can you draw on to help put in proportion how much of an obstacle the rock is?
- What is the satisfaction will you get from overcoming the rock?

5
There has to be an ending before there can be a new beginning

There needs to be closure on the past before there can be a clean new start.

You want to leave a job or a responsibility well with not too many loose ends. You do not want your mind to be cluttered with previous preoccupations as you enter the next phase of your work or life. You list what needs to be finished off and have concluding conversations with those carrying on the activity. You recognise that the final conversation before you move on can be a valuable mentoring conversation. Then you can draw a line and move more freely into the next phase.

Ben was thankful that when he moved into his current role he was able to hand over his previous responsibilities properly. Some tasks had naturally come to an end. In other areas he spent time mentoring and encouraging those now taking forward the work. He needed the satisfaction that he had handed over responsibilities carefully and had engaged in personal development conversations with his key people.

Reflections
- What for you constitutes a good ending that enables you to move on?
- How best do you leave behind thoughts on what you might have done next in a previous role?
- What for you can get in the way of moving on into a new season?

6
A bird's-eye view

Looking from far above a current issue gives you a much wider perspective.

You are immersed in an issue and feel bogged down by the immediate pressures on you. The requests you receive from others feel relentless. There is no hiding place and you cannot see far ahead. You want to look outwards so you can see how others are addressing similar issues and to reflect on how you might engage with others addressing similar problems. You imagine yourself way up above the current issue surveying a wider landscape and assessing how your way of tacking the issue compares with the approach of others.

Ben imagined himself looking down on how he was tackling the issues before him. He could see the journey travelled and the potential routes ahead. He could see how others were tacking similar issues and what had begun to work well or less well for them. He could begin to see an overall destination and the distance that needed to be travelled. All of a sudden, the journey seemed manageable as he had a better perspective on the overall journey.

Reflections
- How best can you lift your perspective beyond the immediate pressures?
- What do you see happening more clearly when you look from high above?
- What insight does this give you about the journey ahead?

7
The next mountain to climb

There is always another mountain to climb so how do you acknowledge and celebrate the journey you have come on so far?

It can be helpful to be thinking about what is the next mountain you want to climb. It can also be daunting and overwhelming to be focused on the next mountain, and then the next mountain to climb. We often don't give ourselves time to celebrate reaching a point where we can look back and see the progress made. We can be relentless in pursuing an ever upward trajectory when we need to stand still and enjoy the progress made and then decide whether we want or need to climb the next mountain.

Ben recognised that he was not good at celebrating progress. He was impatient in wanting to keep moving forward. He had huge reserves of energy, but others in his team were not as bounding in energy as him. Ben recognised that he needed to ensure that each peak reached was celebrated with a full acknowledgement of what each individual had contributed. Ben began to accept that not every mountain needed to be climbed. Some could be circumvented.

Reflections
- How helpful is it to you and others to talk of mountains that need climbing?
- Which mountains might you go round?
- How might others support you in being bolder or holding back when needed?

8
Don't jump over the edge without looking how far you might fall

There are moments to be bold and times to hold back because of the potential consequences of your words and actions

We want to leap in and contradict a developing approach. We are conscious that we do not want to make ourselves unpopular or create a negative backlash. We do not want to create opponents when we will need the support of colleagues for courses of action that are important for us. We initially hold back and decide what evidence we need to support our preferred approach and who might we talk with in order to build a shared understanding about next steps.

Ben had trained himself to look over the edge to see what might be the outcomes if his favoured approach did not work as he had hoped. He asked himself what the consequences might be for the business and his people if decisions proved not to lead to the anticipated outcomes. He was conscious that his personal reputation was such that he could be bold in advocating next steps provided he took key colleagues with him.

Reflections
- How best can you assess the consequences of your recommendations?
- What fears might hold you back from being as bold as you need to be?
- What will enable you not to be fearful of jumping over the edge?

9
Turn the tables

There are moments when truth has to be spoken and drastic visible action is needed so others listen and respond

Sometimes unsavoury or inappropriate actions have become the norm. There is the acceptance of behaviours that are tolerated but are not as they should be. Financial dealings are a bit shady and are tolerated. It is all a bit murky with standards being eroded or semi ignored. Something needs to be said. A light needs to be shone on what is not being done according to the accepted behaviours. Someone needs to speak out. The tables need to be turned so that shady dealings and inappropriate behaviours are revealed.

Ben was concerned that some of his people were taking much longer breaks than they needed to and kept disappearing. Others were working conscientiously for much longer hours than they were being paid for. Ben felt there was systematic abuse of the norms about time and effort put into work. Ben decided that now was the moment to be very clear on his expectations and call out the bad practices that had developed.

Reflections
- What abuses in the way time and resources are used need to be named?
- What can get in the way of your exposing the misuse of resources?
- How might you need to protect some from the insidious behaviour of others?

10
Time to blaze a trail

There are moments when a situation needs you to demonstrate what is possible and not hold back.

The group seems stuck with discussion going round in circles. You are getting caught up in never ending procrastination. You know that something needs to happen and are pretty clear on the right next actions. You decide now is the time to be bold and set out a way forward which you are content to lead. You put to one side your hesitations knowing you have to put forward a confident approach if others are going to follow you.

Ben kept probing away at a project that had stalled. There were various reasons for the slow progress which had sapped the energy and resolve of the team. There were always reasons for further delay. Ben spent time with colleagues on the individual issues and came to a realisation that he needed to advocate more clearly the benefits that would flow from completing the project. He needed blaze a trail about this project that others could follow.

Reflections
- When a group is stuck how might you be a strong advocate about what could be possible?
- When might you personally exemplify the benefits of a particular approach?
- How best do you counter what might hold you back?

11
Every tide has its ebb

However strong a force may currently appear, it is likely to diminish over time.

When waves are pounding onto the beach the relentless force of water seems never ending, but then the apparently unstoppable movement of the water up the beach comes to an end. At times the forces pushing decisions in a particular direction seem relentless but then the advocacy for a particular approach ebbs away and you were glad that you held firm and were not overwhelmed by apparently overwhelming pressures.

Ben was under a lot of pressure to take on an additional project. Ben felt that taking on this additional activity could well overwhelm his team and dampen their ability to deliver on key priorities. Ben surmised that if he could hold back from making a firm decision then, the pressure to take on this project would abate. Ben reminded people of the previous priorities which were critical for the success of the organisation and gradually the pressures for this new initiative began to diminish.

Reflections
- How best do you assess whether what seems like an overwhelming pressure is for a limited period?
- When is procrastination helpful because you judge that the pressures for a particular approach will ebb away?
- When do you judge that you need to move quickly onto higher ground so as not to be overwhelmed by a powerful force?

12
Look before you leap

Seek to be aware of the consequences of your actions so you are not surprised by repercussions.

You can see what needs to be said and done. You have thought through the different arguments and do not want to hesitate about taking next steps, but you recognise that you need to think through some of the consequences before you act. How will different people react and what would be the knock-on effect of saying or doing what you think is the right next step? It might well feel like a leap in the dark but as far as possible you want to judge whether you would be landing on firm ground or be stuck in a quagmire.

Ben could see how a particular type of analysis could enable one of his teams to work more effectively. Ben needed to draw evidence from how other organisations had adopted this approach successfully and what would be the likely reactions of his team members. Ben knew that he needed to be able to tell a clear story about the benefits and consequences before his people would readily buy into the change he was advocating.

Reflections
- What consequences do you hope to achieve from a particular action?
- How best do you build a clear picture about people's reactions beyond the immediate?
- What enables you best to look beyond the immediate reactions?

13
Great oaks from little acorns grow

It is worth investing in developing initial proposals which can lead to effective and sustainable outcomes

You have been investing time into developing an idea or proposition which seems small in itself and modest in the potential benefits, but you recognise that a proposition that is tested and begins to be supported by a cross-section of people can become increasingly accepted as a good way forward. Time is needed for the consequences that flow from the proposition to be assessed.

Ben could sometimes be impatient. He wanted his ideas to catch the imagination and be supported by investment and unequivocal backing. He recognised that decision-making was never straightforward. He needed to ensure that his propositions for future work were well developed and that he caught the imagination of his colleagues about benefits that would flow from the investment of time and energy. He wanted to demonstrate the efficacy of his propositions and the scale of benefits that could follow.

Reflections
- Which ideas do you want to nurture carefully because they have worthwhile potential?
- How do you give yourself space to see what small steps might grow into bigger initiatives?
- How best do you keep your patience as you seek to catch the imagination of different people about what could be possible?

14
Faint hearts never won fair lady

There are moments to be bold in seeking to win the confidence and support of key people.

When are you tempted to be equivocal, ambivalent or even apathetic? When are the moments to put doubts or apprehensions aside and be bold in your advocacy of a course of action? There are moments to hold back and reconsider. There are times when there is a need to leap forward and put your case strongly. There are times when you know you are going to be criticised, but if you don't act you miss the opportunity.

Ben did not engage often with his boss's boss who are preoccupied with a range of different pressures. Catching her imagination was never easy because there was always something more important that she was dealing with. Ben bided his time until he had the opportunity of a short conversation with his boss's boss. He knew that was the moment to be bold in advocating this investment. This was not a time for a faint heart. Ben spoke his mind, got a good hearing and waited to see whether he had been persuasive.

Reflections
- When might you be more faint-hearted than the situation warrants?
- What enables you to switch from faint heart to bold advocate?
- What mindset best enables you to be bolder rather than faint-hearted?

15
A miss is as good as a mile

Realism is important in accepting that a near miss is an unsuccessful outcome.

The harsh reality of life is that if you apply for a job and just fail to get it, you have not been successful. Often in life there are no consolation prizes, you either win or lose. We need to be philosophic when we do not land the outcome we had hoped. We can take satisfaction in just missing an outcome we had hoped for, but then need to move on and recognise that sometimes we are successful and sometimes not, often irrespective of the qualities we bring and the preparation we have put into the task.

Ben recognised that one of his projects had not been successful. He was able to rationalise this disappointment in terms of the learning for his team. He wanted to articulate some of the sustainable benefits, but he knew he should not delude himself or others about the overall success or failure of the project.

Reflections
- How best do you come to terms with relative failure and admit it to yourself and others?
- How best do you balance the relative failure of a project with the benefits that have flowed out of the experimentation?
- When might you be at risk of deluding yourself to view a failure as a success?

16
Necessity is the mother of invention

Necessity brings out a creative and innovative approach to solving problems.

The biggest changes happen when there is no alternative to being creative and working together. Developments in science and technology have often been most significant at times of war when new equipment had to be devised and made quickly. During the Covid-19 pandemic in 2020 barriers broke down and individuals were more willing to work in partnership together to devise new ways of addressing problems. The advance in the use of virtual means of communication accelerated during the Covid-19 lock-downs and created a pace of change that nobody had ever envisaged would have been possible.

Ben received a very clear message from his boss that the financial viability of their organisation depended on finding a breakthrough in tackling a particularly intractable issue. Ben recognised that he needed to put his best people into tackling this issue and empower them to be inventive in experimenting with different ways of looking at the problem to try and find a feasible way forward.

Reflections
- What brings out the most inventive in your people?
- How do you create a sense of urgency which forces and legitimises colleagues going into inventive mode?
- What are your best examples of necessity being the mother of invention?

17
One swallow does not make a summer

Early indications are always helpful but do not guarantee success.

We welcome encouragements and initial signs that progress is being made. One voice of encouragement can lift our spirits. A risk is that we take too much account of lone voices which may not be indicative of a broader reaction. On the other hand, individual comments of affirmation can give us indicators that we are making progress and that there is a reasonable prospect of a successful outcome.

Ben was always looking for indications that his projects were meeting with approval. He recognised that some individuals would always say nice things to him at an early stage in order to keep him happy. He recognised that other people needed more evidence before they would affirm what he was doing. He was judicious in the way he both recognised milestones being reached and at the same time, and recognised the continuing progress that was needed. It was important to him to spot indicators of progress and be able to build on them without assuming long-term success was inevitable.

Reflections
- What are the indications of progress you are most looking for?
- How best do you affirm progress without assuming inevitable success?
- How best do you ensure you do not waste too much time looking for the first swallow?

18
Beware of the battle of the egos

It is best to watch from the side-lines when a battle of egos is playing out.

Some people like the sound of their own voice and always want to be right. Putting two people with these characteristics in the same group can be a recipe for discord unless there is clear contracting about appropriate behaviours. When two people are battling it out, you probably don't want to get caught in the middle and want to wait judiciously until they have either resolved the problem or you can enter with a conciliatory approach or an alternative direction.

Ben found it exhausting to be in disagreement with some of his peers. He watched some of the more senior people in the organisation become ever more emotive when they were trying to resolve a way forward on difficult issues. Ben recognised that he needed to wait for them to become tired of arguing which would then give him the opportunity to advocate a way forward that would not have received a warm reception at an earlier stage.

Reflections
- When might your ego get in the way of reaching an agreed outcome?
- How best do you handle a situation where two people with big egos are at loggerheads with each other?
- How do you temper your own approach when you feel you have the right answer?

19
A chain is only as strong as its weakest link

If one bit of your enterprise is not as robust as it needs to be the whole enterprise's reputation can be tarnished.

Which bits of your organisation are robust and can cope with external shocks? How ready are people to step into the shoes of others and ensure sustainability when dealing with unexpected absences? It is worth stress-testing different parts of your organisation to build a picture of where there is resilience and where there is fragility.

Ben was conscious that he needed to keep a careful eye on the resilience of each part of his wider team. He was conscious that the organisational resilience would be lowest when there were absences, or new appointees, or people in post who were focused on future opportunities rather than their current role. Ben would score what he judged as the resilience of each part of the organisation out of ten and keep a record of his personal assessment. This provided a prompt for him about where he needed to focus his attention.

Reflections
- What for you distinguishes a weak link from a strong link?
- How much investment of your time should go into addressing weak links?
- How adaptable is your organisation so the weakness in one area can be accommodated by a strong input from another area?

20
A journey of a thousand miles begins with a single step

Once you make your first step you are on your way to travelling a long distance.

The first step is often the most difficult one to make. You have weighed up the pros and cons of a particular action and you are clear that you are travelling in the right direction. As you take the first step you are apprehensive but also believe that you can make sustainable progress. You get into a rhythm and enjoy the initial progress while recognising there is a long way to go. The seemingly unattainable begins to look possible.

Ben had weighed up carefully whether his team had the capability to take on a big, long-term project. He had wrestled with the uncertainties and risks before committing his team to deliver a project that would take many weeks to complete. He knew he needed to stop procrastinating and take a decision to proceed and put in place the first steps. Once he did so his confidence in the whole endeavour shot up.

Reflections
- How helpful to you is it to view a project as a sequence of doable steps?
- What helps you take the first step when the goal is a long way off?
- How open are you to have very long-term aspirations that will take many steps to reach?

21
A picture is worth a thousand words

Many people absorb and retain ideas more effectively through pictures than words.

Your eyes glaze over when reading a page packed with words, but a diagram or picture catches your imagination and you understand the concept that a mass of words are trying to elucidate. A diagram can show the interlinks between different factors which take many words to explain. A picture can evoke an emotion which sums up a message you are trying to convey. It is always worth asking what is the diagram or picture that sums up your message.

Ben wanted to depict convincingly the outcomes from a particular planned project. A description in words was fine for some people, but he needed to catch the imagination of those whose support he particularly needed. He created a simple diagram to illustrate how the eventual project would operate. He wondered whether it was too simplistic to include an illustration of people with a smiling faces enjoying the outcome from the project. He decided he would take the risk of being seen as a bit gimmicky in illustrating the project result.

Reflections
- When has a picture or diagram convinced you that a proposed action is right?
- When you write text is it worth thinking about what diagram or picture might accompany that text?
- When has an accompanying picture undermined a proposal?

22
Don't kill the goose that lays the golden egg

Financial realism can mean continuing with the dull rather than the interesting.

The search for the new can mean that the stability and financial income that is generated from well-established products and services can be undervalued. In any enterprise it is worth reflecting on what continues to generate an important income stream that needs to be nurtured. Who are the core funders of a charity or the regular purchasers of products and services who need to be recognised and not dismissed as irrelevant or out-dated?

Ben was conscious that some of his people did valuable, routine work for clients with the risk that he ignored their efforts. He needed to keep reminding himself that they created a regular funding stream that allowed other people to take forward new initiatives. When senior people in the organisation questioned whether the routine work was adding to the business, Ben was assiduous in pointing out that the income stream that flowed from this routine work provided the core stability enabling new ideas to be taken forward elsewhere

Reflections
* Which bits of your enterprise are you at risk of undervaluing?
* How do you link the focus given to particular areas with the income flow they generate?
* Who do you need to regularly affirm who is delivering routine, underpinning contributions to your enterprise?

23
Look beyond the end of your nose

There is always the risk that we focus on the issues immediately in front of us.

Our minds can be filled with the daily expectations and the emotions that result from short-term pressures and expedience. Looking to the future gets squeezed out and there is never enough time to think about the long-term consequences of actions. We risk being blind to the longer-term attitudinal and behaviour changes we are influencing in others by letting forceful people dominate our agenda. As we look forward beyond the end of our nose, we see the twists and turns ahead of us and are better prepared for them.

Ben felt he was always battling with the Finance Department who wanted short-term return on investment. He had to keep repeating the message that the projects were about long-term behaviour change which would lead to a good financial return. He had to hold back his impatience sometimes when there seemed little recognition of the need to identify long-term behaviour change that would flow from effective project implementation.

Reflections
- How best do you set aside time to think through long-term consequences of your actions?
- Who can you best talk through long-term consequences with?
- How best do you control your patience when the relentless focus is on the short-term?

24
The immediate can drive out the important

We can be slaves to doing immediate tasks.

E-mails flow into the inbox and we feel a duty to respond. We get into a relentless round of immediate responses which can dominate our time. Perhaps there are moments in the week or the day when we can stand back and reflect on what are the important tasks that we need to focus on rather than the immediate. Perhaps it is useful to grade at the start of each week what is in the important category and commit some time to address those, even if it means disappearing from view.

Ben was always being chased to sort out immediate issues. He set aside time when he might disappear in order to work on some urgent and important topics while always ensuring that someone in the Department was available for the immediate request with a clear brief to sift out when something was genuinely immediate and when it could take its place alongside other priorities.

Reflections
- How can you ensure you balance out a focus on both short term goals and longer term vision?
- What helps you sift out the important from the immediate, and give enough time and energy to the important?
- When can you disappear in order to focus on the important?

SECTION B

Values

25
Hope springs eternal

There always needs to be the hope that there can be something better going forward.

Even when you feel at your most dejected, can there be a sense of hope that life could get better? Out of the darkest times can come opportunities. Hope keeps us going even when the current situation feels dire and relentless. Perhaps we can see hope in people's faces or draw from the experiences of other people going through tough times who have been able to keep their resolve in the midst of continuous setbacks. Without any sense of hope, we sink into a quagmire of despair.

Gillian worked as a senior member of a staff association representing senior groups of staff. She felt passionately that organisations ran more effectively if the views of employees were taken carefully into account. If often felt that the door was being slammed in her face by the senior management of the organisations she was seeking to influence. What kept her going was a passionate belief that the voice of employees needed to heard. When she felt ignored by management, she knew that she had to keep cheerful and positive.

Reflections
- When does the sense of hope keep you going?
- How best do you keep up a belief in hope when the door is slammed in your face?
- How does the sense of hope keep you grounded?

26
A close shave

At times we have to recognise that we are close to a potentially dangerous situation.

There are moments when we push the boundaries and argue a case that is not necessarily supported by others. We make a decision without fully getting backing from key people and are ready to ask for forgiveness having not asked for permission. We enter a negotiation and concede more than our bosses might have wanted us to concede. We recognise that we could be criticised but are deliberate in exercising our own judgement.

Gillian often felt in an exposed position when she negotiated with employers. She was balancing the interests of those people she was representing alongside seeking a pragmatic outcome. Sometimes she knew she would incur the wrath of her members, and on other occasions the employer would be thinking she could deliver more. Gillian recognised that she was doing a balancing act and having to be mindful when she was at risk of not being able to carry the support she needed or deliver what she had implied was possible. It could feel like one close shave after another.

Reflections
- How far are you willing to push the boundaries in negotiations?
- When are you willing to ask for forgiveness rather than permission?
- How best do you handle criticism that you have let others down by not getting the outcome they wanted?

27
Life is a roundabout

Arguments and people may keep circulating without moving forward.

Sometimes you feel that arguments are circular with no progress. The same people keep appearing, maybe with different responsibilities, but making the same arguments. Little progress appears to be being made. When do you try and push the roundabout faster, or get off the roundabout, or seek to persuade others that the relentless journey around and around is resulting in no progress? Sometimes we have to accept that there is circularity of argument that needs to continue until the players get exhausted or significant new information is available.

Gillian recognised that she was likely to hear the same arguments repeatedly from employers for not increasing flexible working arrangements for employees. Different HR people arrived on the scene and parroted the same points. Gillian was persistent in trying to find examples of where staff flexibility had been good for both the organisation and the employees and judiciously used these examples to try and overcome the very conservative inhibitions. She became immune to the circularity of negative argument and was gradually able to deploy examples of successful initiatives.

Reflections
- Can you smile at the repeated parity of the same perspectives?
- When have you been able to break through a circular argument with new evidence?
- How can you work with others to break through circular arguments?

28
The dog that didn't bark

Where a point is not made it often means it is less important than you had initially thought.

Sometimes a matter that has been a preoccupation quietly disappears. Perhaps it has been resolved or the players consider it to not be as important as they had previously implied. Earlier priorities can often get overlaid by new imperatives. It can be helpful to review why a particular issue had not come to the fore when previously it has been seen as contentious. Such reviews can provide good insights about what is most significant going forward.

Gillian was conscious that some issues were matters of continuous concern, but other issues would be significant one week and would then disappear from view. When she talked with different groups of her members, she noticed what was not raised as much as what was raised. If she then raised the unspoken issue, she would often be told that it continued to be a priority, but its absence was a good indicator of relative priority.

Reflections
- How helpful is it to observe what topics are not raised as concerns?
- How long might you let an issue be talked through before you judge whether it is an on-going concern or is going to fade away?
- When do you quietly forget what had previously been a significant preoccupation?

29
Keep watch

It is always worth keeping alert to how ideas and inter-relationships are developing.

How much do you gain by observing what is happening in a meeting or how different parts of a negotiation are playing out? We learn as much by watching as doing. Seeing the interplay of people in a meeting can be very instructive as you watch for the appropriate moment to interject. Keeping watch includes bringing a sense of anticipation about what might happen next and how best that is interpreted. Being open to see the unexpected is key to being watchful.

Gillian had trained herself to watch people's physical and emotional reactions carefully. She could sense when she was on a good point that was being processed carefully, or when she was being given the standard line. She watched for the moment when she could put a proposition forward because it now met an objective that was important to the organisation she was negotiating with. There were moments to leap in with a very clear proposition, but for most of the time Gillian listened carefully and was then ready to make a measured intervention.

Reflections
- What enables you to watch a meeting carefully?
- What can get in the way of you being watchful when you are engaging with others?
- What helps you get you timing right in terms of when you intervene?

30
Know when to keep our distance

There are times when maintaining your independence is key so you are not captive to any particular viewpoint.

Your views might be being sought so you are seen as backing a particular proposition. You might have an alliance with a colleague who wants to assume that you will support an approach they are putting forward. You recognise that there is a need for a quick decision but you are determined not to be forced into a premature view before you have properly considered the evidence.

Gillian was for ever being lobbied by individual members to advocate their cause. Often, she was convinced by their case and she would be unequivocal in her support. On other occasions she was conscious that the individual was putting forward special pleading which was not convincing. On these occasions Gillian was judicious in her use of language in setting out the case of the individual while not wanting to use her personal capital to advocate a case about which she was not fully convinced.

Reflections
- Beware least people associate you with a particular viewpoint about which you are not fully convinced
- Be ready to sit lightly to a particular viewpoint if you think that there needs to be new evidence to fully inform next steps
- Follow your intuitive sense about how closely you associate yourself with a particular approach

31
The elephant in the room

There are times when an issue is too difficult to tackle and is not spoken about.

A group of individuals can readily get used to working around an obstacle to the extent that the presence of the obstacle is not spoken about. The obstacle might be the fixed views of one individual, an assumption that a particular outcome would never be acceptable or a financial issue that feels too difficult to tackle. Progress may well never happen until that obstacle is named and addressed.

Gillian built her reputation as an honest and capable negotiator by being deliberate in pointing out a perception or historic consideration that was acting as a massive inhibitor to progress. Gillian had developed an approach of naming a difficult issue in a measured and yet sensitive way. Gillian's technique was not to express blame: her approach was to be factual about naming obstacles and inhibitors, and seeking an open discussion about what possibilities might there be for making progress.

Reflections
- When is it helpful to reflect on what are the unnamed issues that are influencing behaviours and decisions?
- How best do you draw attention to unspoken truth that is influencing everybody's attitude?
- When is it best to keep working round an obstacle and accept that now is not the right time to point out the unspoken truth?

32
Bury the hatchet

There are moments to move on from the pain of disagreement and find a constructive way forward.

You might have had an intense disagreement with a colleague. You felt they had used evidence in a misleading way which had damaged your working relationship. You felt trust had been eroded, but you knew you had to keep working together. An element of resentment is unhelpful and getting in the way. You recognise you have to move on and build a constructive, forward relationship. You identify a couple of issues where you need to work jointly with this colleague.

Gillian recognised that she would have to express views forcibly in some situations when management was not listening. Her members expected her to be clear, direct and forceful. Gillian also understood how important it was to keep positive relationships with people in management responsibilities with whom she was going to have continuous dialogue. Gillian knew she had to keep these relationships in a professional space. She had to put on one side feelings of being misrepresented or misunderstood.

Reflections
- What can help you be bold in drawing attention to uncomfortable truths?
- How helpful is it to you to use the language of burying the hatchet?
- What helps you build constructive relationships with those with whom you have had fundamental disagreements?

33
Draw the line

There are moments when no is the right answer.

When you are being pushed continually in a particular direction your patience can run dry and you need to be unequivocal in saying that you have come as far as you are going to move in a discussion or negotiation. There may be issues where you are asked to present something in a way in which you do not think is a fair reflection of the facts and you believe it is right to draw the line about what can be said in a particular situation.

Gillian knew that she had to advocate the cases put forward by her members but there were moments when she felt it necessary to be clear to her members that a case was so weak that it was not worth taking forward with management. Gillian needed to build credibility both with managers and with employees which was partially based on them all recognising that she would draw a clear line if she thought that an argument was untenable and unsupported by the facts.

Reflections
- How do you hold your ground when you are being pressured to take a course of action you do not agree with?
- What helps you balance different perspectives while being authentic to your own position?
- What helps you come through a situation where you need to draw a line?

34
Face the music

There are times when you need to accept that you have been responsible for a mistake and then face the consequences.

You took a decision with the best of intentions. You had sought to weigh up the evidence carefully but unfolding events meant that the desired result did not happen and you did not deliver on the expectations. Perhaps you acted too hastily or did not take into account key factors that might have shaped your perspective. You are honest about what you did and what went wrong and are clear about your learning. You accept there will be some criticism but accept that that is life.

Gillian recognised that her members could, at times, be emotive. There would be occasions when they felt she had let them down by not getting the outcome they thought they were justified in receiving. She recognised that the critical comments were an expression of frustration about the situation and were not a measure of whether she was effective in her job or not. But it could be painful when she was subjected to a barrage of negative comment.

Reflections
- When things go wrong under your watch, how readily do you take responsibility?
- What helps you come through a situation where you are held responsible?
- How best do you retain your authentic self when you are accused of failing?

35
Don't waste a crisis

When a crisis happens, change is always accelerated.

When you are in the midst of an apparent crisis it is always worth trying to stand back and reflect on what is happening and whether there are going to be opportunities that flow from the turmoil that a crisis creates. Previous work practises have been changed quickly in a way that had never previously been thought acceptable. A crisis can mean that dialogue happens in a frank way between people who had previously been at odds with each other. A crisis can mean a burst of new energy to solve what has seemed insurmountable problems.

Gillian relished a crisis. She thought quickly and could sense when there might be an opportunity to work together with previously difficult managers. Financial reductions in a particular area inevitably meant that management had to take difficult decisions about deployment and potential redundancy. At these times Gillian knew that managers may be more open to changes to working practises as part of an overall deal or understanding. Gillian kept being alert to possibilities however difficult a crisis situation became.

Reflections
- How best in a crisis do you create time to think about what opportunities it opens up?
- What are the trade-offs that can come to the fore when there is a crisis?
- Can you allow yourself to enjoy a crisis?

36
People in glass houses should not throw stones

Beware lest you attribute faults to others that are equally your failings.

We hold someone else to account for not delivering in a particular area when we may not have fully delivered all we were expected to contribute. We can see faults in others but are blind to our having the same characteristics. We regard someone as talking too much in meetings when we also like to contribute on every item. We can be blind to how we can annoy other people and benefit from feedback from trusted others so we are able to more readily modify our interventions.

Gillian often thought that the people she was negotiating with were intransigent and blinkered and liked to think of herself as modelling adaptable behaviours with a willingness to be flexible in finding constructive ways forward. She recognised, however, that she had to be careful when she wanted to describe someone as intransigent as she was conscious that the same criticism could be levelled at her. She sought to defuse situations by openly acknowledging that others could regard her sometimes as intransigent.

Reflections
- When might you criticise others for faults you also have?
- How best do you get feedback so you are conscious of when you might be applying double standards?
- How might you depersonalise comments so they are independent observations rather than personal criticism?

37
We have two ears and one mouth

It is worth listening for longer than you speak.

Active listening involves hearing the words, observing the emotions and recognising the underlying interaction between different concerns. The best of leaders are always listening and refining their thinking in the light of what they hear. Words are chosen carefully so as to steer conversations and to elicit information and understanding. With trusted others we talk through ideas with a listening ear so we are continually refining our understanding. Key is listening to hear the underlying issues and emotions rather than just the presenting issue.

Gillian recognised that she needed to understand the views of a myriad of different people before she settled her on her negotiating position with management. She needed to listen carefully to the managers she was going to negotiate with so she understood both the deliberate and the unconscious signals about priorities. She tried to focus her interventions on key questions and concerns to help steer and not dominate discussions.

Reflections
- How might you listen more actively?
- When might you ask a question rather than offer a definite view?
- When might you ask a question rather than offer a definite view?

38
None so deaf as those who will not hear

Be wary of those who are determined not to hear or take account of what is being said.

A colleague might look as if they are listening but you question how much they are hearing. As you speak, they are nodding at the right points. You try to elucidate their reaction by asking about their observations on what you have said and soon sense whether you are getting platitudinous comments back or whether they are engaging with the concerns you express. You search for a point of connection and wait to see if there is any animation in their face.

Gillian got used to glazed looks from those she was engaging with or polite smiles. Gillian recognised she had to start with a point of common interest in order to build rapport and interchange before she got to a point that she particularly wanted her interlocutors to hear and take account of. Before each meeting Gillian would ask herself, 'how do I need to express a viewpoint in a way that is going to ensure that it is heard and taken account of?'

Reflections
- How best do you assess whether someone is hearing as well as listening?
- What might attract the interest of someone who you want to engage with?
- Which trusted others can help you both talk and listen in tricky situations?

39
Connect brain to mouth

Beware lest your words fail to align with where the brain wants to take you.

Sometimes the brain is active and buzzing making lots of good connections, but the mouth stays shut because of a lack of confidence or opportunity. Sometimes words pour out of our mouth in an incoherent way as we work out what we think. We may need to talk an issue through before we know what our brain thinks, but need to be wary about the signals we are giving to others when we are exploring ideas. Sometimes we need to shut up to let our brain process its thinking before we speak.

Gillian recognised that people she dealt with would often be talking at her for a period before they had connected their brain to their words. Gillian was conscious too that she could use the same technique when she was working out what she really thought about an issue. Gillian was always impressed by people who could align their words with the thinking in their heads.

Reflections
- When do you need to keep talking in order to work out what your brain thinks?
- How might you sometimes slow down your brain so that your words can catch up with your thinking?
- How tolerant do you need to be when someone's brain and mouth are not connecting?

40
No smoke without fire

When there is disturbance it is always worth seeking to find out the cause.

When something goes wrong our reaction might be 'who is to blame?'. There is a risk that we assume that an initial indication of a problem means that there is something flawed about the whole enterprise. As we delve into the issue, we may find that the forewarning about something going wrong has been a useful indicator but that the spark that caused the problem might not be the fundamental problem.

Gillian always took seriously concerns expressed by individual members of staff. When they expressed a comment there would always have been a reason. She recognised that sometimes the cause was significant and on other occasions it was random and incidental. Gillian knew she needed to triangulate with trusted others to assess whether or not there was a significant and underlying problem.

Reflections
- When there is an indication of a problem how open-minded are you in assessing the cause?
- What stops you from jumping to criticisms before you have assessed the reasons for a problem?
- Is your risk to intervene too quickly or too slowly when there is an indication of a problem?

41
Once bitten twice shy

When you have felt misrepresented there is a natural wariness.

You start off by assuming trust until trust is broken. When someone uses data you have given them to further their own ends or misrepresents what you have said, you feel hurt and let down. You become wary of them and manage much more carefully what you say to them and how you engage with them. The risk is that you stand back too much when what is needed is your continued engagement with these people who you feel have let you down, while seeking to minimise the risk of you being misrepresented or being taken for granted.

Gillian built up a perspective about whose views and commitments she could trust and who she needed to be wary of. Sometimes employees were fearful of telling her the whole truth while managers wanted to protect their own position and minimise Gillian's influence. When Gillian felt her trust had been abused, she needed to treat that as data to influence the way she engaged with others and not to feel resentful about their behaviour.

Reflections
- How do you respond if you feel someone has misrepresented you?
- How do you ensure that when you feel let down that you continue to engage in a constructive way?
- When do you deliberately withdraw and bide your time?

42
Silence gives consent

Watch the risk that your absence of comment implies agreement.

In a world of rapid e-mail traffic absence of comment can be implied as assent. Often, we need to talk to people directly to understand whether they are at one with our way of thinking and to glean whether they have a perspective that needs to inform our favoured way forward. In any group there needs to be an accepted way in which people can express reservations or ask for further time to reflect and comment.

Managers would often assume that if Gillian did not respond in the moment that she endorsed their way forward. Gillian learnt that she needed to be deliberate when ideas were floated by her about when she was being supportive and when there needed to be further evidence and clarification before she was able to reach a definite decision. Often at the end of a meeting she would summarize what she had agreed and note what she was considering further in order to avoid the assumption that her silence meant consent.

Reflections
- Be wary when your silence might be interpreted as consent?
- Seek to build an understanding of where decisions are made so that silence in response to an e-mail is not misinterpreted?
- Don't let the assumption build up that you agree if you do not reply instantly to an e-mail?

43
Don't feel you have to fill the silence

It is fine to leave silence to allow you and others to think through an issue.

There are few things more irritating than people who keep talking. A consequence is that others get bored or feel they have to jump in and talk at an equal length with a resulting. cacophony of voices and absence of progress. A good Chair will slow a meeting down to allow moments of reflection and silence. Silence can create golden moments as we crystallize the way we think about a way forward.

Gillian recognised that silence was a valuable part of her negotiating approach. In anxious moments she knew there was a risk that she would want to fill the silence. She had learnt over time that it was often best to leave a gap after making a comment or asking a question allowing moments of silence while waiting for others to fill the space. Often break throughs in negotiation took place when Gillian had held the silence long enough for others to feel obliged to set out a way forward.

Reflections
- How comfortable are you holding silence and waiting for others to comment first?
- When has your silence led to a breakthrough in understanding by those you are engaging with?
- How can you best develop an instinct for where it is critical that you voice your opinion?

44
The least said the soonest mended

Sometimes it is wise not to comment when emotional reactions are preeminent.

We have all observed situations when in the heat of the moment things are said which would have been better left unsaid. Emotive reactions generate more emotive reactions with a mild disagreement escalating into a major dispute. Words that are said in anger cannot then be unsaid. The damage done can often be permanent with relationships scared for ever. Words said in the heat of the moment can have a far more devastating effect than ever you anticipated.

Gillian felt that she needed to be constantly tempering her comments with an eye to maintaining long-term working relationships. She kept holding onto her prime objective which was to ensure that significant forward progress was made in key negotiations with her recognising that things that were said in the heat of the moment by others provided her with useful data about points of anxiety, but were rarely things that she should immediately respond to. She recognised that she needed to be careful that her emotions did not lead to comments she would subsequently regret.

Reflections
- When you feel anger, how do restrain yourself?
- What enables you to hold back from saying what you think are perfectly justifiable reactions?
- What enables you to focus on the long-term relationship and not on a particular incident?

45
Truth will out

The true facts in any situation will eventually emerge.

You sense that all the evidence is not available. You seek to find out the perspectives of a range of different people and not jump to conclusions about what is the truth in a particular situation. You hold the firm belief that over time more evidence will become clear that will enable the true facts to be seen in a more coherent way. You recognise that you have to live with partial information and trust that the decisions you make will be regarded as the best ones you could have made in the circumstances when comprehensive evidence was not available to you.

Gillian felt that she was repeatedly being told partial truths by both the employees she was representing and the managers. She was hearing about disagreements and disputes that had got out of hand. She sought to focus on what were the key facts that had led to disagreement or acrimony. She had trained herself to bring a forensic approach to distinguish between fact and emotion.

Reflections
- How readily do you start from the evidence rather than a perception about what has gone wrong?
- How best do you build partnership with others to seek the objective truth in any situation?
- When might you be blinkered to the underlying reasons for a problem?

46
Truth has many dimensions

There are always various ways of seeing reality.

What is seen by one person as truth is viewed by another as prejudice. We see each situation through the lens of our experience and personal frames of reference. Being blinkered in our perception of reality can sometimes be helpful in enabling us to focus on what most needs to be done, but an excess of singlemindedness means that we can become blind to alternative views of reality. It is always helpful to see the world through different lenses to our own.

Gillian was acutely aware that an irrefutable fact for one person was conjecture for another. What was self-evident truth for an employee, was viewed by managers as a blinkered and isolated perspective. She was often saying to her members that it is important to see situations from the perspective of those who are focused on the future of the organisation. She knew she had to sit as lightly as she could to the strongly held views of some individuals because they were always going to be coloured by their own personal circumstances.

Reflections
- How do you best look at an issue from someone else's perspective alongside your own?
- Who helps you understand different perceptions when there is a difficult negotiation?
- In what situations do you believe there is only one version of the truth?

47
Watch getting steamed up

Feeling strongly on an issue gives us energy but we can distort our judgement.

When we feel strongly on an issue and don't feel we have been taken seriously, we can feel frustration building up inside. We want to express that frustration by speaking or writing strongly on a subject. We are at risk of showing anger rather than understanding, and of being forceful rather than measured. A sense of indignation can be helpful in building up a determination to make change happen. What matters is how we focus that indignation so that we choose words and contexts that are going to make the biggest difference.

Gillian could find herself burning with frustration when she observed gross misunderstanding or manipulation. Destructive behaviour was destroying goodwill. She knew she had to stand back when she felt frustrated and be deliberate in how she managed her interventions. She knew she had built up capital with a range of different managers and could influence them to change their minds. She needed to be energized by the unfairness she saw but then focus her frustration and only annoy people when she deliberately chose so to do.

Reflections
- Keep observing your inner barometer.
- When you begin to feel worked up, how best do you keep being deliberate in your responses?
- Who can you share your sense of frustration with who will calm you down?

48
Be mindful if you are giving the cold shoulder

We can inadvertently be giving negative messages to people.

We build up a rhythm over time of how we engage with people in different contexts. We may depart from that rhythm because we are focusing on a particular issue without appreciating that our change of rhythm is being perceived adversely by others around us who begin to feel rejected and irrelevant. Key is seeking to keep a realistic rhythm of engagement with different people, and explaining why we are focused on aspects that are predominant for us at the moment.

Gillian was conscious that she was balancing the interests of many different members who wanted more of her time than she could reasonably give. When she did not respond instantly to their e-mails, they could easily feel that she was dismissing their concerns. Gillian learnt that she had to be deliberate in describing in what circumstances she was available to people and that they should not take silence as her ignoring them.

Reflections
- How can you best balance being available to others and focusing on your key priorities?
- In what situations are you at risk of seeming to ignore others?
- What works for you in reassuring people that you are still interested in what they are doing when you have to focus on other things?

49
Actions speak louder than words

Supportive actions will be remembered for much longer than bland words.

Acts of kindness may seem incidental but are often remembered for years ahead. Taking on someone's responsibility when there are domestic issues or overwhelming priorities will be long remembered: these supportive acts will shape the reputation that you build up. Action to stop agreement being reached on something when key colleagues with different views to yours are not available speaks volumes about your belief in fairness. Enabling your team to help support another team at a tough moment will be remembered for far longer than your comment that the other team seems under a lot of pressure.

Gillian enjoyed using words be it in writing or orally. Her fluency had enabled her to influence many managers over recent years. She was always persuasive and influential, but at the root of her influence were her small acts of kindness. She recognised when people were struggling and needed support. She was generous inviting people for coffee and giving small gifts. She knew when a helping hand was needed to enable someone to cope with a difficult situation.

Reflections
- When have you been influenced by small acts of kindness that have shaped your attitude to individuals?
- When are actions more important than words in influencing others?
- What acts of kindness might you do over the next week?

50
All that glitters is not gold

An apparently attractive way forward may not have as many benefits as first anticipated.

A colleague advocates an approach forcefully eulogising about the benefits. You warm to their enthusiasm and find yourself predisposed to wanting the outcomes they have set out persuasively. You remind yourself that reaching those outcomes might not be as straightforward as your colleague is suggesting. You want to be enthralled by possibilities and look at them seriously, but you accept that sometimes you need to hold back your enthusiasm until the route to the desired outcomes is clearer.

Gillian started with a degree of scepticism when an employer announced that they were proposing new employee benefits that would change significantly their work experience. Gillian knew that she would need to look beyond the glowing words into the content of what was being proposed. She was not going to be bamboozled by rhetoric while recognising that positive words from management about staff wellbeing were to be welcomed as she could hold them to account if the promise turned out to be greater than the actuality.

Reflections
- What helps restrain you when an offer looks overwhelmingly good?
- How best do you hold onto the enthusiasm of advocates whilst testing the robustness of what they are proposing?
- When might you be at risk of over emphasizing the attractiveness of a particular route?

51
As you sow so shall you reap

There are always consequences from our actions that cannot be ignored.

Most words we say or actions we take have consequences. When we suggest an idea, it will be influencing others, even if the impact is purely that their belief in their preferred way forward is reinforced. If we sow discord it can readily lead to major disagreement. On the other hand, if we bring a sense of compassion that will legitimise compassion in others. The demeanour we show others will frequently result in our colleagues showing that same demeanour to us.

Gillian recognised that when she showed frustration it led to a higher level of frustration being shown by others. If she brought a desire to work together, her approach was more likely to be replicated by those with whom she was engaging. Gillian recognised that she had a powerful influence through the tone she set as many people would mirror her demeanour. She would choose her moment to indicate her willingness to compromise and when to be deliberately intransigent, knowing that others would be likely to respond in kind.

Reflections
- How deliberate do you want to be in the ideas you sow?
- What helps you be patient in observing which ideas you sow germinate and flourish?
- How readily do you recognise when people re sowing ideas for your benefit?

52
Watch if familiarity breeds contempt

Be mindful about when openness can be counterproductive.

We all need people with whom we can share our deepest concerns. When we have vulnerabilities working them through with a trusted colleague can help us address apprehensions and overcome inhibitions. But there is a risk in personal disclosure as it means that others see our failings and more readily observe when we are at risk of manipulating a situation or misusing the authority we have. It is worth keeping an eye out for situations where someone loses respect for you because of the way you have disclosed your own weaknesses and uncertainties.

Gillian recognised that some of the managers she was dealing with wanted to build a friendly rapport with her. She was wary about how much she shared about the issues she was facing and did not want to talk about her particular anxieties. Gillian wanted to keep these relationships at a professional level: she recognised that if a manager shared too much about their own uncertainties, it might lead to her not considering the points the manager made as seriously as she should.

Reflections
- How do you keep relationships professional with a good level of rapport without becoming over familiar?
- At what point might you lose the respect of someone you are engaging with?
- When can losing respect lead to conflict?

53
You can't make a silk purse out of a sow's ear

There are times when you need to recognise that you do not have the evidence to reach sound proposals.

You want to find a way forward but the evidence base is not strong. There are some results from attitudinal surveys alongside a variety of strongly held views. You accept that you may be criticised if you do not propose a precise, well thought through option. You have to recognise that all you can put forward are some hypotheses based on limited evidence. You have to accept that you will disappoint those people who are looking to you for a definitive solution.

Gillian knew that if she was going to win an argument with management then she would need evidence and not just hearsay comments about the possibilities. She often concluded that there was no point in putting an argument to management until better evidence could be put together. This frustrated her members who always felt that she could convert their desires into a convincing narrative.

Reflections
- When do you need to accept that your evidence base provides an inadequate rationale for your favoured approach?
- At what point do you stop putting together a case you don't believe in?
- How willing are you to disappoint people when the evidence you have is unconvincing?

SECTION C

Value-added

54
A foot in the door

Making an initial intervention means your viewpoint is more likely to be considered.

Sometimes discussion is flowing and you are not sure how to break into a fast-moving conversation. Perhaps you might ask a question, or elaborate a point someone else has made. Emotionally you are feeling excluded and are at risk of coming over in as anxious. You know you have to select an instant when you can make one comment to show you are engaging. You want your comment to appear useful or you might be at risk of being shut out.

William knew he could appear a bit anxious and uncertain with a resulting risk that he could be ignored. It was not William's inclination to dominate conversations, but he could sit back for too long. He recognised that one observation about potential consequences of a particular decision was all that was needed when a conversation was in full flow. He did need to ensure that people recognised that his was a contribution that should not be ignored.

Reflections
- What type of intervention works best for you when you are at risk of feeling ignored?
- How best do you hold back until an appropriate moment to intervene?
- When might personal anxiety hold you back from intervening at the right moment?

55
The first rocks in the jar

When you define your first priorities it becomes clearer what room there is for other activities.

When choices need to be made about the use of time and energy it is helpful to reflect on what are your major tasks. When the scope of these tasks has been established it is much clearer what time and energy can be available for other activities. There is always a risk that we start off by committing ourselves to a diverse number of activities which then constrains the time available for important work and personal priorities.

William liked having chats with members of his staff as keeping in touch with them helped build up goodwill. William recognised from previous experience that he had to be disciplined in saying to himself, "what are the key activities on which I will be assessed and where I can add most value?" This question helped him focus on key activities first and then be available for informal conversations at times of day when he needed a break from his core activities.

Reflections
- When you start a new month, are you planning to put the right rocks in the jar first?
- How best do you ensure you focus on the tasks where your value-add is going to be greatest?
- How do you time limit the activities that are of value but ancillary to your prime focus?

56
Build on rock and not on sand

What is the firm base on which you want to build so it provides a firm foundation?

It is always worth reflecting on how secure are the foundations on which you are seeking to build. Assumptions about how people are going to react in different situations might need to be reassessed. Previous patterns of behaviour may not be replicated. You need to establish what are the most likely reactions to proposals based on current rather than dated evidence. Are the financial assumptions flaky or robust? Do influential people think your assumptions are sound or wayward and inconsistent with the evidence?

William had a keen eye when assessing underlying facts. He was willing to make himself unpopular with his colleagues by saying that a particular suggestion was inconsistent with the evidence base. He was assiduous in putting together key facts before putting a proposition to the Executive Team. He knew from previous experience that when his analysis was not robust, he would fail to gain the agreement of his colleagues.

Reflections
- How best do you judge whether you are building on rock or sand?
- How best do you assess how strong the foundation is for your suggested way forward?
- How far do you admit that the foundations for your argument are limited?

57
The hoop you have to jump through

Sometimes there are approval mechanisms that are unavoidable.

Identifying all the approvals needed at the start can seem daunting and even depressing, but once there is a forward plan you can best judge how an argument needs to be presented if it is to win the necessary sequence of approvals. You can then see the progression of next steps. It can feel like an unnecessary activity to have to jump through hurdles but the process of defining the argument so it can be explained coherently to others is invaluable.

William brought a long-term perspective in the way he advised others about leading projects. He recognised that an approval process could seem daunting but suggested there were benefits from having to put together a clear narrative and then subject it to scrutiny from different perspectives. Going through an approval or review process was never wasted as far as William was concerned, provided it was possible to keep a clear focus on the intent of the endeavour and the benefits that would subsequently flow.

Reflections
- What enables you to view a necessary approval as an opportunity to crystallize your rationale?
- Can you see the need to jump through a hurdle as part of building a coherent narrative?
- Can you push back when processes become too bureaucratic?

58
Three steps forward and two steps back

When we make progress, we sometimes have to consolidate that progress before we can move forward.

We may have thought we had won an argument and that others are aligned behind our proposition but then feel that others are chipping away at progress we have made and forcing us to backtrack on certain aspects. We observe ourselves going on the defensive and seeking to protect the progress we have made. We are philosophic in recognising that sometimes progress comes through a forward leap which is met by pushback, with overall some net progress.

William thought he had been successful in persuading his people about the benefits of a particular course of action. Over the next couple of weeks doubts were raised and some of the benefits seemed less attractive than initially assumed. William felt he was being pushed into retreat but recognised that overall, he had made some progress in changing attitudes in favour of a particular course of action. He knew he had to regroup and reframe his plans for the future.

Reflections
- Can you be philosophic about the reality that progress will sometimes be three steps forward and two steps back?
- What helps you recognise when pushback is based on evidence rather than emotion?
- How can you express your arguments soundly and thereby reduce the likelihood of successful pushback?

59
Go slow to go fast

There are times when we need to wait patiently.

We observe animals moving slowly and choosing their moment to pounce and catch their prey. We may feel that we have the ideal solution and want to present it early and persuasively. Sometimes we need to wait until others are exhausted before we set out a way forward. We need to wait patiently for the moment when people are ready to listen to us and are not going to dismiss what we say. We may need to be firm with ourselves and others that patience is key for long-term success, and that at the right moment we will take action.

William as a Senior Civil Servant had worked with a range of different Government Ministers and recognised from experience when was the right moment to put forward an unwelcome proposal. The way resources were being used were not having the outcomes that were most needed. William had evidence about relative cost effectiveness but knew that Ministers were wedded to certain ways of doing things so he had to be careful in choosing his moment in advocating shifts in funding arrangements.

Reflections
- At what point do you say now is the time for action?
- How best do you keep patient and gradually build support from others?
- What can result in your rushing into decisions too quickly?

60
Be careful what you wish for

We want action to be taken forward but might then find ourselves responsible for their delivery.

We long for an opportunity to influence key decisions. We would love to have the flexibility to make choices about relative priorities and believe we can make choices much more effectively than other people who currently hold those responsibilities. When we see the need for changes to happen it is sometimes helpful to think ourselves into the situation where we could influence those actions happening and then decide whether we would welcome taking on that responsibility or not.

William was often frustrated by decisions Ministers had taken and was sometimes inwardly critical of the ability of his colleagues to persuade Ministers of necessary action. William was asked to lead a major urgent project which included regular conversations with the Minister. He could not now complain about the advice going to Ministers. He was in pole position giving advice and, therefore, was carrying exactly the responsibilities that he had expressed a desire to be given.

Reflections
* How readily would you take on the responsibilities of people who you are currently critical of?
* How open are you to the possibility that you might have opportunities beyond what you might now see as possible?
* What would help you stop wishing for things that you are not suited to take on?

61
Steering not rowing

Every venture needs to be successfully steered.

For a boat to reach its destination it needs to be successfully steered. That might mean a gentle shift in a modified direction, or it might mean a fundamental change of direction. Effective steering depends on looking ahead and seeing potential obstacles and identifying the most effective forward course. Good quality and persistent rowing is necessary to keep forward movement, but without wise steering the energy going into the rowing is dissipated. The value-add that comes from careful steering helps to maximise the impact of the energy of those people seeking to drive the enterprise forward.

William kept needing to remind himself that his role was to steer and not to row. He had lots of willing staff committed to the success of the enterprise. They relied on William to be navigating them through choppy waters where they were facing criticism from a variety of different sources. It felt as if there were often forces pushing the team in the wrong direction with William having to carefully navigate a pathway to ensure that progress was forwards and not backwards.

Reflections
- How readily can you leave rowing to others and keep your focus on steering a way forward?
- What enables you to steer well through choppy waters?
- What type of communication works best between those who are rowing and the person steering?

62
Armed to the teeth

Effective preparation increases the likelihood of success.

Experience might have taught us that we need to be prepared for criticism so we are less likely to become defensive when we are accused of not having thought through issues effectively. We need to be prepared for attacks from the front which we can see coming and sometimes criticism from the side or behind us which catches us unawares. When putting ourselves into an exposed position being ready for counter-arguments as well as insidious reactions from both critics and so-called neutral parties or expected supporters, can stop us from being disorientated by unhelpful reactions.

William knew from bitter experience that he needed to be well prepared for appearances before Parliamentary committees. He needed to have thought through the issues they might raise from different angles. He also had to be prepared to address the reactions from colleagues in his own organisation if he didn't present the Department's case as powerfully as they would have liked. William accepted that he had to be prepared to respond to a raft of different questions most of which would never get asked.

Reflections
- How best do you prepare for what might be a critical reception?
- What are the risks of over preparing so you don't feel too weighed down?
- How best do you prepare yourself for potential criticisms from both opponents and so-called supporters?

63
Lion-hearted

There are times when boldness is demanded.

The situation has drifted for quite a long time. Someone needs to be bold and grip this situation. Someone needs to shape the arguments into a coherent narrative with a clarity about what needs to be the outcome and what steps need to be taken to get there. A leader needs to emerge who is adventurous and willing to stake their personal reputation on a course of action. Sometimes it falls to you to be the person who is willing to be frank, bold and visible in advocating next steps.

Nobody was volunteering to have the tough conversation with a colleague who was a cause of irritation through their manner and disdainful behaviour. William was willing to have the difficult conversation and risk a barrage of criticism and resentment. William prepared himself for the difficult conversation and knew he needed to be bold. In the event the colleague readily recognised how annoying they had been and promised to try and shift their behaviour. William and his colleagues waited to see if this intent was going to be delivered.

Reflections
- When do you need to be bold and risk your own reputation?
- How best do you build alliances when you need to say unpopular things?
- When might boldness veer into foolhardiness?

64
Wait till the clouds roll by

You need to allow time for moments of gloom to pass.

When travelling on a long walk you want the dark clouds to pass by as quickly as possible. Sometimes they roll by unabated and you have to be patient. Eventually, you see the edge of the clouds and a shaft of sunlight beginning to burst through. As the clouds eventually pass now is the moment to celebrate and see the views that had previously been hidden. Now is the opportunity to encourage others to look forward to distant outcomes that had been hidden and seemingly unattainable.

William sought to bring a cheerful disposition into every conversation. When there was gloom or pessimism, he did not want to bring a false optimism which he knew would not help the situation. But there would always be a sense of hope and possibility in how he viewed the future. He drew from past experience in reminding his colleagues that storms never lasted for ever. There was the prospect of moving forward as dark periods were moved through and signs of progress began to appear.

Reflections
- Which clouds have recently rolled by and are now in the past?
- How do others view the way you handle dark clouds?
- How do you best prepare for the moment when clouds have passed and a clear lead from you is needed?

65
Soaring and swooping like an eagle

Looking down from above helps you decide when to intervene.

On country walks near where we live, we often see red kites who soar effortlessly in the sky and then swoop fast to catch their prey. As they circle around, they are keeping a close watch on movement below ready to see an opportunity and then intervene. When we are in the midst of activity there are moments when it is good to seek to understand what is happening from a wider perspective and then be mindful of when we might intervene with an action or observation.

William was conscious that some of his people wanted to develop their independence of thinking and did not want him intervening on a regular basis. William recognised that standing back more was the right approach to developing their self-confidence and decisiveness, but he always sought to keep a careful eye on what was happening and then be deliberate about moments when he intervened. He was not going to abdicate his accountability for ensuring action took place, but he was going to be selective about when he offered a comment.

Reflections
- What helps you soar above an issue and see the wider connections?
- How best do you decide when to soar and when to intervene?
- How selective are you about the ways in which you swoop and then withdraw?

66
Keep your powder dry

Deploy your evidence when it is going to have its biggest impact.

You may have found a key piece of evidence but are conscious that you need to deploy that information at a point when it is going to have its greatest impact. Contributing too early, and you may not be listened to. Intervening at a late stage might mean that the opportunity has passed to change the direction. You want to be selective in deploying information in a way which will be listened to and regarded as helpful. At a moment of uncertainty your contribution can be invaluable. When someone is in full flow, your contribution might be dismissed as an irritant.

William had new information that could change the direction of a policy. The dilemma was did he share this information now or did he wait until there was further evidence which reinforced this initial information. He knew he had to have a coherent evidence-based argument but also knew that he would be regarded as acting in bad faith if he did not share his intelligence at an early stage

Reflections
- When might you be inclined to rush in with a half-substantiated point?
- What helps you be deliberate in when you deploy new evidence?
- What can help you stop delaying when you want to intervene?

67
Nip in the bud

When action is required quickly, careful judgement is needed about what ideas are to be taken forward and which are to be dismissed immediately they have been spoken. A clear sense of prioritisation can sift good from the indifferent ideas. On some occasions an idea needs to germinate and be explored before it can be assessed as either worthwhile or irrelevant. Articulating why an idea is being dismissed straightaway is key to avoiding the criticism of being blinkered.

William was working with a Minister who had lots of ideas. William recognised that his people would not be able to handle the welter of ideas the Minister was coming up with. William recognised that he needed to be very open with the Minister in prioritising which ideas were to be taken forward and which would be set aside. William brought humour in teasing the Minister about their welter of ideas and working through with the Minister which ideas should be taken to the next stage.

Reflections
- When someone comes up with a new idea, is your natural inclination to explore it or dismiss it?
- How best do you prioritise between different ideas all of which are being strongly advocated?
- What is the rationale you use when you have to dismiss ideas because of the need to handle other priorities?

68
The early bird catches the worm

Being willing to explore new ideas and opportunities at an early stage is rarely wasted.

It can be helpful to be seeking to spot trends and to recognise where there might be new opportunities. How might a new market be opening up, or new technology meaning there is greater scope for innovative thinking? Who are the opinion-formers or innovators it is good to be engaging with so your eyes are open to possibilities and you can initiate exploration or action at an early stage?

William had worked with a sequence of different Government Ministers and had learnt that it was important to listen to them attentively early on in their tenure to understand what they preferences and inclinations were. Early, open conversations always gave him a good feel for how best to work with them to engage with their imagination and build a strong bond of credibility and respect. When anything untoward happened William knew that he needed to be alongside the Minister at a very early stage so that they were working through a problem together and not in isolation.

Reflections
- Listening to what is going on at the earliest possible stage always gives new insights?
- Scanning the horizon for new problems or opportunities is never wasted?
- Being curious what is beginning to appear on people's forward agenda gives valuable intelligence?

69
Strike while the iron is hot

There are moments when you need to make the most of an immediate opportunity.

When a conversation has run its course or a dialogue has got stuck, there can be a moment of uncertainty or silence when you can intervene to maximum effect. Setting out a precise summary or a clear, forward direction spoken simply and confidently can turn a conversation from looking down with gloom to looking forward with optimism. Key are words that are forward-looking and catch the imagination, and a demeanour that looks as if you believe what you are saying and have credible evidence to support your proposals.

William knew that his Minister was devasted that he was not getting the support he wanted from his own party colleagues on a particular initiative. William commiserated with his Minister and decided to advocate a variant which would meet most of the Minister's concerns and be more likely to be well received by the Minister's colleagues. William chose his moment carefully and after some irritation the Minister put forward a new approach that was largely based on what William had suggested.

Reflections
- Be ready to seize the moment when it is offered to you?
- When your opportunity comes, be clear, direct and not hesitant?
- Once you set off with a clear proposition don't be put off it there is an element of surprise?

70
Keep the pot boiling

There are times when you need to ensure that the creative energy addressing a particular area is maintained and not dissipated.

There have been good conversations on an issue but other things are distracting people. You use a mixture of encouragement, flattery and practical incentives to keep the focus on forward thinking and detailed exploration of different solutions. You are relentless and disciplined in your approach while being sensitive to how people are reacting emotionally to your steering of conversations.

William recognised that the Minister would not let go on a particular point. William's immediate reports in this area were feeling weighed down by other priorities and not keen to come up with any new ideas. William recognised that he needed to keep talking with his people in an encouraging way whilst being very clear in his expectation that a couple of new, worked-up proposals needed to be with the Minister within two to three weeks. William prompted a sequence of conversations and was clearly not going to let go of this issue until clear proposals had gone to the Minister.

Reflections
- When might you need to be bold in ensuring that focus is retained an a key issue?
- How do you best respond when someone seeks to distract attention from a problem?
- What allows you to be resolute your own reputation being undermined?

71
Take the bull by the horns

There are moments when you have to deal decisively with a difficult issue.

When a way needs to be found going forward in addressing a particular issue, what can stall progress is disappointment about the lack of forward movement, boredom amongst the participants, niggles that are getting in the way and other priorities where forward action is more obviously needed. There are times when you have to be relentless in ensuring a conversation continues.

Savings needed to be found in a particular part of the organisation but no-one was prepared to move: the underlying rationale was the assumption that the problem would eventually go way. William chose his moment to bring people together and began by affirming them and illustrating the progress made so far. He then encouraged the sharing of new ideas and repeated that work needed to continue on this issue until a solution was found. The team recognised the truth in these comments and knuckled down to find a way forward.

Reflections
- How best do you ensure that you do deal decisively with an issue that is causing pain?
- How do you stop yourself getting bored or disappearing when an issue needs to be addressed?
- How best do you keep a dialogue going when other participants want to disappear?

72
A cat may look at a king

However junior we are we can learn by observing those in leadership roles.

We are on a continuous journey learning from those people we are observing and engaging with. Sometimes viewing them with admiration and on other occasions with scepticism. We need to look with discerning eyes as we decide whose perspective we believe and who we are sceptical of. However important someone is we bring our own discernment in judging their impact on others and on us. We can be conscious of the filters which might blur our perspective about how someone is living their values or creating the impact that they are seeking to achieve.

William felt privileged to be in regular contact with Cabinet Ministers. He was impressed by their speed of thought, but sometimes concerned about their fixation on particular presentational considerations. He developed a mixture of respect and wariness, knowing that his reputation with Ministers was only as good as the quality of his last intervention on their behalf.

Reflections
- How best do we observe a leader objectively without being prejudiced in their favour or against them?
- What helps open our eyes to qualities we had not previously seen in a leader?
- What can overawe us about a leader which means we are blind to their faults?

73
Make hay while the sun shines

There are moments when we can make a lot of progress: go for it.

We may find ourselves in favour with the current leadership. An event may have gone well under our watch and we observe that our credibility and authority is at a high level. We have started an initiative which is going well and there is a momentum that we can reinforce that is going in the right direction. We need to accept that now is the time to make progress recognising that it will not always be this way. Our champions may move on and circumstances may change.

William had helped the Minister refine an approach which had worked well. William observed that there was goodwill towards him at the moment and recognised that this was the moment to try to reach a conclusion on a couple of issues that had stalled. William recognised that he had a window of opportunity that he needed to be unhesitating in taking.

Reflections
• Be willing to recognise when your approach is being favoured and think through how you build on that predisposition?
• Be ready to surface issues that have got stuck when you sense there is goodwill on your side?
• Beware less you hold back too much in moments when you have more influence and authority than you might immediately realise?

74
Know the ropes

It is important to know the boundaries within which you are operating and to understand the way things are done in an organisation.

You may feel that you have a lot of flexibility and can take forward a range of different ideas. But what are the boundaries of acceptability and pitfalls? Sometimes you want to push the boundaries but it is always worth knowing what the assumptions are about acceptable ways of working so that you can be deliberate in deciding when you want to operate within accepted norms and when you want to push to see what shifts in the way things are done you can prompt.

Because William had done work within Government over a couple of decades, he understood what approaches were most likely to work. But he wanted to push himself and others outside their comfort zones and be more creative in their approach. He knew that he needed to cultivate champions who would support him in trying new approaches. Gradually he shifted people's perspectives so they became more willing to try creative approaches.

Reflections
* How well do you understand what are assumed to be the acceptable ways of doing things in your organisation?
* How best do you shift people's perceptions about working in different ways?
* How much can you be a role model in helping others push the boundaries in terms of taking forward new approaches?

75
Half a loaf is better than none

There may have been limited progress, but there has been some forward movement.

We have set the intent of winning support for a new approach and have established reluctant part acceptance. Our initial reaction is one of disappointment rather than satisfaction that we have made some progress. We recognise that we need to work through that disappointment to reach the point where we can acknowledge that progress has been made and that we have a new base on which to build.

William sought to persuade his Minister to engage directly with a wider number of officials using the argument that it was more helpful for the Minister to hear directly from the officials dealing with a particular subject rather than talking to an intermediary. William was initially disappointed about progress but recognised that there had been some shift in the Minister's approach. William concluded that he needed to move forward in stages and affirm the progress the Minister had made rather than be overly disappointed.

Reflections
- What enables you to be satisfied when you have only made half the progress you had wanted to make?
- How do you set your aspiration so that getting halfway there is still a big achievement?
- When should you be dissatisfied with making partial progress?

76
Fortune knocks once on every door

Sometimes you have an unexpected opportunity: take it.

A string of different decisions may not have gone your way and you think your career is moribund. But you then have a new boss who sees the potential in you and is advocating your cause. There can be a moment in time when an opportunity opens up. We can be caught by surprise and think that our good fortune is not real. We need to accept that sometimes an opportunity arises or a door opens and we need to move forward positively believing that there is a moment in time when we can confidently embrace new possibilities.

William had never expected to be promoted to the Executive Group. He was loyal and hardworking, but did not see himself as exceptional. But his thoroughness and careful weighing of possibilities had enabled him to build a strong reputation. He had built the confidence of successive Ministers. He was told that he was on the succession plan to join the executive team when the next vacancy arose.

Reflections
- How do you respond when an unexpected opportunity opens us?
- Are you willing to accept that sometimes good fortune will come your way?
- How best do you keep up your resolve when everything seems to go contrary to your best interests?

Two heads are better than one

Working closely with a trusted colleague or partner can give valuable insights.

When I was the Finance Director for a Government Department, I often worked collaboratively with the HR Director and as a result of joint working we brought the best out of each other. I have written books and booklets with a number of co-authors with joint analysis of the issues enabling us to prepare content that was far better than either of us would have produced individually. Often talking through a difficult issue with a colleague enables new angles to be explored and fresh solutions examined.

William was good at working in partnership with key colleagues. When there was an issue, he would identify who would be a good sounding board with whom he could work through the approach and risks. He was always willing to spend time with colleagues helping them work through complicated issues. He thereby built up a set of reciprocal and mutually reinforcing working relationships that enabled him to reflect on progress and next steps.

Reflections
- Who might you partner with to work through difficult issues?
- How best do you build up mutual mentoring so that the benefits are two-way?
- When do you accept that you have to make a decision alone and that further dialogue with others is not going to clarify your thinking?

Too many cooks spoil the broth

Too many people involved in decision-making can slow the process and dilute the outcome.

There is a delicate balance between involving a wide range of people in decision-making and keeping the final decision-making to a focused group of people. Too many people thinking they have the right answer can cause delay, disappointment and mistrust. Being clear at what stage and for what reason people are involved and clarifying where final decisions are made, can build necessary realism. There is a moment to say we understand where people are coming from, but we now have to limit the decision-making to a small group.

William was naturally democratic and open. He wanted to engage people right across his Directorate which was spread over a number of sites across the country. Consequentially decision-making in his Directorate became complex and overburdensome. He knew he had to simplify the governance structure and make himself unpopular with some people for a period. He recognised he had to be clear in his approach and explain his reasons simply and deliberately.

Reflections
- When has involving too many people in decision-making diluted the impact you wanted to achieve?
- What is the right balance in your situation between open consultation and decisive action?
- How best do you explain not involving someone when you know this will be a disappointment to them?

79
A stitch in time saves nine

Identifying an issue early significantly reduces the amount of time and energy needed to finding a solution.

It may be helpful to review periodically what are the niggles that are causing irritation. Are there ways in which these niggles can be addressed so that they don't escalate and become a case of major discord? We want to tell ourselves that time invested in addressing an embryonic problem is never wasted, but in a fast-moving context we don't necessarily believe our own advice.

William sensed there was the beginning of a breakdown in relationship between two of his direct reports. They had seemed to rub along fine for the last year, but he detected a bit of passive aggressive behaviour creeping out. William deliberately took them both out for coffee and began to chat through with them how they could bring the best out of each other. They recognised the risk of a deteriorating relationship and committed themselves to keeping talking to each other to ensure the working relationship was enhanced and not diminished.

Reflections
- When might an early intervention help reduce the possibility of discord?
- What can get in the way of an exploratory conversation when you recognise that an issue could gradually escalate unhelpfully?
- What examples can you hold in your mind of where early intervention has proved to be useful?

80
Be alert to the domino effect

Be conscious of the knock-on effect of everything you say and do.

A good leader knows that a suggestion made to one influential person will pass rapidly around an organisation. An insensitive leader may not recognise that a critical comment will circulate quickly and either generate a constructive response or a sense of resentment and distrust. A moment of panic travels like wildfire and is soon contagious. Just as one domino can knock over a row of dominoes quickly, so one ill-judged comment can damage trust and shared endeavour fast. Equally, good gossip engenders goodwill and a sense of mutual support far more effectively than you might realise.

William recognised who were the opinion formers in his organisation and ensured they were conscious of good news or areas where new thinking was needed. He was also aware who were the inveterate gossips with whom he needed to be especially mindful about what he said to them as he knew they would magnify and megaphone his comments emphasizing the negative rather than the positive.

Reflections
- Who do you share good news with knowing that it will be passed on?
- Who are you wary of sharing your frustrations with because they might magnify them?
- How might you use the domino effect constructively in sending messages around an organisation?

81
Put your best foot forward

Know what is the relevant experience you bring and draw from it.

We can be at risk of being too modest and feeling that others are better at handling difficult or unexpected situations. What experience have you had from the past that is relevant that you can draw on? Key is starting with the mindset that there is something distinctive you can bring, however unpredictable or unprecedented the situation. With that positive mindset and a belief that you can contribute, it is quite likely that your intuitive reactions will be of value and will not be dismissed.

William was conscious that something had gone wrong under his watch. He knew he must not wallow in disappointment. He needed to think clearly about how best to rescue the situation and move it forward in a way that was convincing to his Minister. He ensured that a clear rescue plan was put together by a team leader who was well regarded by the Minister. He asserted confidently and convincingly with the Minister that a difficult situation could be overcome with minimal damage.

Reflections
- What enables you to be bold when you need to rescue a situation?
- What can hold you back when you need to use your strengths and experience confidently?
- When do you need to be uninhibited in being a bold advocate?

82
Seek to ensure both ends meet

Be watchful when you initiate thinking from two different people that this does not lead to conflict or discontinuity.

You may ask one person to start with the detail and another to reflect on the wider trends. You want each of them to work cognisant of what the other person is doing so that the contributions they offer provide complementary perspectives. You are conscious that people can become so preoccupied with their individual activity that they lose sight of how different elements connect. Your regular refrain is about what the ultimate goal is and how the different activities complement each other.

William was conscious that good officials will be seeking to draw conclusions from the evidence they were dealing with, whilst not always recognising that they bring their own mindset and sometimes prejudices. William also recognised that the Minister viewed everything from a political lens and was conscious how any step would be perceived both in the media and public opinion. There was inevitably a risk of jagged edges and misunderstanding.

Reflections
- How best do you ensure that when people start with different perspectives that they keep talking to each other?
- How readily do you foresee potential conflict when people are working to different rather than similar ends?
- Might you need to communicate more fully when you set people off in two complementary directions?

83
Among the blind the one-eyed man is king

You may feel that your clarity of vision is limited but others might be even more blinkered than you.

You can quickly feel uncertain if you have only a dim insight into next steps. The resulting risk is that you close in on yourself and do not offer a way forward, even though others have less understanding than you, however confidently they talk. You sense there are three or four key factors and you seek as confidently as you can to crystallize those points in speaking up. You are then surprised that you have helped shape a forward discussion about next steps.

William could sometimes forget how much his experience in different situations had shaped his understanding. His intuitive reactions were well tuned because of working with a wide range of different Government Ministers, including one who had gone on to be the Prime Minister. Sometimes he would steal himself in a situation of uncertainty to set out a clear proposition and would be surprised by his own influence.

Reflections
- Recognise that your limited understanding might be much greater than those around you
- Be willing to set out a limited number of key points based on your understanding and observe how those are received
- Accept that sometimes your authority and influence can be greater than you expect

84
Better late than never

Sometimes it is better to produce a quality product late than an inferior product on time.

Some deadlines are unavoidable. Sometimes a deadline needs to be negotiated so that a product is robust and sustainable. The risk of a precise, unchangeable deadline can be that if it is not met energy and commitment fall away so no outcome is produced, and motivation collapses. The mindful leader is watchful about when deadlines are motivational or destructive. There is a measured skill in modifying deadlines so that reasonable expectations are met, and motivation and commitment are maintained.

William kept a watchful eye on the expectations of his Minister and the work of his staff. The Minister wanted a new funding model in a particular area: officials were working diligently on new approaches but were having to wait for key information. William had to manage the expectations of the Minister that he would need to wait a bit longer to get a quality product. He was also managing the motivation of the officials to ensure the product was fit for purpose while not needing to be perfect.

Reflections
- When do you need to be rigid about deadlines?
- What guides you when you decide to flex a timetable?
- How best do you manage expectations when something is going to be delivered later than desired?

85
Discretion is the better part of value

There are moments to favour caution over rash boldness.

You may feel you have had a long tussle with an individual or pressure group and you have had a successful outcome. You want to celebrate and are tempted to emphasise your victory alongside the defeat of others, but you will still need to work with these people going forward. There is no need to keep exclaiming that you won and they lost. There will be occasions when you will have shared interests so now is not the moment to be highlighting your victory and their defeat.

William had advised his Minister against saying something highly critical about a pressure group. The Minister had not heeded William's advice and had taken great pleasure in saying how inept this organisation had been. William wanted to be direct with the Minister about what he saw as a counter-productive approach. He held back because he anticipated that the Minister was likely to recognise before too long that he needed to build an alliance with this organisation on points on which they were in agreement.

Reflection
- When might you be at risk of gloating about victory?
- What enables you to hold back from criticising others when they are likely to learn their own lessons without your intervention?
- How best do you see discretion as a strength and not as an avoidance tactic?

Be on the balcony and on the dance floor

Being part of the action and looking from the wider perspective gives you in combination a valuable overall insight.

Being amidst the action gives you an understanding of the pressures, dynamics and struggles. Looking from above enables you to understand the trends and overall movements, as well as seeing local action in a wider perspective. The risk is we spend too much time either floating above an issue or stuck in the detail. The value-add we bring can be because we appreciate the interaction between the immediate action and the overall pressures, expectations and wider consequences.

William recognised that one of his roles in the Executive Team was to bring a perspective about what was happening in local areas. At the same time, he recognised he needed to keep looking ahead and be thinking through how resources could be used best to enhance the scope for putting technical education higher up the Government's agenda. He recognised that his crusade in favour of technical education needed to be grounded in solid evidence about economic benefits.

Reflection
- How best do you ensure you get the right balance between understanding the detail and bringing a wider perspective?
- How best do you justify to yourself spending time away from the detailed action in order to bring a wider perspective?
- What helps you stop becoming too embroiled in day-to-day action?

87
Use the long screwdriver occasionally

There are moments when you need to delve into the detail to satisfy yourself that appropriate action is taken.

One CEO I worked with was criticised for 'using the long screwdriver' and delving too often into the detail. He maintained that the periodic use of the long screwdriver was how be built up an understanding of what was happening deep in the organisation. The occasional detailed exploration helped him stay realistic, focused and bold. His credibility depended not only on his wider perspective, but on his grasp of seemingly intractable problems.

William rationed himself to becoming involved in the detail of a troublesome issue about once a month. When he did decide to immerse himself in a detailed issue he would always explain why and commit to his involvement being for a short period. He was conscious that this approach could mean that people wanted to dump difficult problems on him, hence his deliberate rationing of the occasions when he would do a deep dive. William was very sensitive to the amount of time and energy he focused on this type of activity.

Reflections
- Recognise when and why you have a desire to go into the detail?
- See a focus on detail as part of your repertoire of approaches, but keep its use in proportion?
- Communicate clearly why you are involving yourself in the detail?

88
A germ of truth

When you feel unfairly criticised there may be a germ of truth in what is being said.

When someone feels that the feedback, they have received is unfair and unwarranted I might ask them what is the germ of truth in what is being said. Often feedback says more about the giver of the feedback than the recipient, but there are normally elements or indications within what is said that is worth thinking through. The truth that may need to be addressed is the perception of what you offer rather than the actuality of what you have done.

William often had to listen to entirely predictable speeches from pressure groups. William had taught himself to focus on weighing up what were the nuggets in what was being said that he needed to take seriously and seek to address. Sometimes the key issue that he needed to consider was the big presenting issue, but often it was some detailed points that needed to be considered further rather than the big, controversial presenting issue.

Reflections
- What enables you to recognise a point of substance amidst a deluge of rhetoric?
- How best do you record and take forward a new thought amidst a deluge of predictable words?
- What enables you to sift out key points from otherwise sterile debates?

Conversations in the grey space

Unattributed conversations in a private space can sometimes release a way forward.

Some discussions need to be formal and on the record. They are a statement of positions as much for a wider audience as for the immediate recipient of eloquent sentences. Often real progress is made in a private space where options can be talked through without an audience. Informal discussion about pros, cons and risks can help build mutual understanding and trust if there is a shared desire to find a way forward. Such conversations often shift perceptions and lead to a greater realism in finding ways forward that can be accepted without anyone feeling humiliated.

William recognised that a particular interest group was influential with their leader being able to get coverage for any of their complaints. On sensitive issues William did not want there to be a public slanging match. He had got to know his interlocutor well and built a mutual understanding about when they were talking on the record and when they were talking in an informal and non-attributable way.

Reflection
- Who do you trust well enough to have open, non-attributable conversations with?
- How best do you balance progress through formal means or informal conversation?
- How best do you ensure that there is a good level of trust and that your openness is not being taken advantage of?

90
Three strikes and you are out

Making one mistake is acceptable, two is admissible, while three might be unacceptable.

We can learn as much from our mistakes as successes. What matters is how we embed the learning from mistakes. We recognise that repeating the same mistake has consequences. We need to be deliberate in learning from the initial mistake with our learning reinforced by a second similar error, recognising that making the same misjudgements three times can be terminal in terms of our reputation.

William had underestimated the significance of a particular issue to a previous Minister and had not fully recognised how, after two mishaps, he needed to invest in ensuring that a third did not happen. Having learnt from this experience William was meticulous in ensuring that lessons were learnt when things had received the ire of his current Minister. William's approach was now always to explore how to increase the prospect of success going forward rather than apportioning blame to what might have happened in the past.

Reflections
- When are you at risk of being a touch blasé when mistakes have been made?
- How best do you ensure that there is a rigorous process of learning from things that have not gone well?
- What personal capital are you willing to deploy to ensure that something does not go wrong three times in a row?

91
Be ready for the wake-up call

An event or comment can surprise us or shock us and lead to new thinking.

We think we are on a clear way forward. We have thought through the opportunities and risks and have a clear plan, but an adverse reaction jolts us into recognising that we need to think again about our approach and how best we take forward our intent taking account of the unexpected and unpredictable. We are awakened from a degree of complacency knowing that it is dangerous to assume that we always know the right answer.

William was an experienced leader who thought through issues carefully and drew on a sequence of trusted advisors. He had not anticipated that one ally would suddenly become a major critic. William felt initially resentful about this change in approach but came to accept that this individual was setting out genuine concerns that William needed to address. He came to accept that he had become a shade complacent and that he needed a wake-up call to think afresh about some approaches that had worked before but might not be quite as appropriate going forward.

Reflections
- How have you received wake-up calls in the past?
- What type of wake-up call are you most receptive to hearing?
- Who do you want to encourage to give you wake-up calls?

SECTION D

Vitality

92
Put a tiger in your tank

Sometimes energy needs to be focused on one intent drawing on your reserves.

There are times when action is needed quickly. You have to focus and be relentless. You know that you have to think and act fast and recognise that you cannot hold back. You tell yourself that this is going to be tough, relentless, exhausting and potentially enjoyable. You know that you will not be able to keep up this same momentum for a long period, but for a defined season you recognise that this commitment, drive and forward momentum is essential.

Saira got a buzz out of intense activity. No problem was too big to solve. She moved towards problems that needed sorting rather away from them. With relative ease she could move into the mode of thinking quickly and decisively. She relished working with others who were operating at speed. Intense activity brought out the best in her, but Saira was conscious that while she could operate at high speed for a significant period, there were risks for her if the speed and pressure were unabated.

Reflections
- How do you respond to intense pressure?
- What enables you to think and act quickly when that is needed?
- What are the risks for you when you go into intense activity at high speed?

93
Don't hit your head against a brick well

There are times when an objective is not attainable and you need to change course.

You are determined to make a success of a particular enterprise. You have invested a lot of time and energy and see failure as not an option. You have been relentless in persuading others of the merits of your approach and the attainability of the outcome. When obstacles seem unassailable you go into persistent and indefatigable mode. There is a point where you have to accept that you are not going to make progress and you have to withdraw and reassess what might be a more effective and sustainable approach to addressing a blockage.

Saira's mentality was that rules were there to be overcome. She was not easily defeated or pushed back. She had a track record of overcoming blockages and obstacles. Saira was conscious of this reputation and did not want to let herself or others down. Over time she became better at recognising when to accept that a different way had to be found.

Reflections
- When are you at risk of repeating yourself to no good effect?
- When is it better to withdraw and find an alternative way round a blockage?
- What has been your learning from previous occasions when you have persisted too long with an approach that was not working?

94
A walk in the park

Sometimes an activity can be less exhausting than you had previously anticipated.

We can sometimes find ourselves in a pattern of dealing with a particular issue and not using too much nervous energy in taking it forward. Reminding ourselves that we enjoy certain activities can help us use those activities to relax our body, mind and heart so we are able to conserve energy for when we go into more demanding situations. Describing activities at work that we enjoy as being akin to a walk in the park reminds us of the pleasure we can get from certain areas of work.

Saira was a great encourager. She spotted when her staff were good at moving forward action and influencing others. Saira enjoyed mentoring others: this energized her and enabled her to feel that she was making a helpful contribution to others. For Saira having a mentoring conversation enabling someone to think through how they tackled a problem was as energising as a walk in the park in allowing her to feel cheerful and positive about her colleagues.

Reflections
- What particularly relaxes you in your work activities?
- How do you create time for these activities that relax you and enable you to feel cheerful?
- What lifts your spirits most in the work context?

95
Walk before you can run

There are times to hold back and ensure you are fully equipped to take on new responsibilities.

We can be so enthused by a new responsibility, task or skill that we want to be operating at high speed quickly. Another part of us wants to move forward in a more measured way. gradually building up our competence and confidence. We need good friends and colleagues to say, "take it gradually, build up your experience and then steadily take on more responsibility". You are told to not rush your next steps for fear of falling over. You recognise the truth in this advice, but want to press ahead.

Saira had joined a very different organisation in an influential role and saw how she could make a significant difference. She brought a fast mind, understood the problems and saw solutions. She knew that she would need to refine her understanding before her sensitivities would be acute enough to be able to develop and advocate sustainable ways forward. She kept wanting to move quickly but knew she had to hold herself back sometimes.

Reflections
- When are you at risk of wanting to move too quickly?
- What could help you build up your experience and expertise so you can have a decisive effect going forward?
- When do you need to slow yourself down?

96
Take deep breaths

Slow yourself down by taking deep breaths.

You are living on the edge of your nervous energy. Your mind is racing. Your heart is pumping quickly. You recognise you need to stop, quiet yourself and take some deep, long breaths. You might take deep breaths as you move around or even in the midst of a meeting you may use deep breathing as a means of settling yourself and changing gear in a way that your brain is racing ahead and needs to calm down.

Saira had a very quick brain and had a reputation for acting and speaking fast. She found it difficult to restrain herself when action was happening quickly. She always wanted to be up there fully engaged and influential. Taking deep breaths and seeking to calm herself down did not come naturally to her. She needed to walk away from intensive action in order to breathe deeply, or if she was in a meeting, she would deliberately and quietly take a deep breath and observe how her body and her emotions settled.

Reflections
- How do you recognise when you need to calm yourself and take some deep breathes?
- What enables you to go into a frame of mind where you can take deep breaths?
- What can happen if you do not give yourself the space to take some deep breaths?

97
What goes up comes down

Excitement can build up quickly about a particular venture, and then dissipate equally quickly.

Media interest in a particular subject can fluctuate as journalists clump around a particular issue, and interest can wane just as rapidly as journalists rush to cover the newest story. You may be delighted by the interest shown in your area and recognise that you need to build on that engagement to create a momentum that will continue when the focus of attention has moved elsewhere. You may be the flavour of the moment one day and ignored the next, even though your approach and output has not changed.

Saira saw her reputation rise with one CEO as a consequence of the way she dealt with some tricky issues. A new CEO arrived with their own advisors. Saira was not consulted as much and felt that her influence and reputation had dropped She was the same person giving the same advice but she had come to recognise that you may be taken seriously one day and become more peripheral on the next day through no consequence of your own actions.

Reflections
- Seize the moment where you can.
- Accept that reputations rise and fall without the individual doing anything different.
- Use the moments well when you feel in the ascendency.

Show a clean pair of heals

Press ahead with action that is needed when you have the opportunity to do so.

There are moments when we are given an opportunity or we see an opening that we need to take full advantage of. An influential person is willing to listen to our views so we take full advantage of the access to them. There are opportunities to take forward new initiatives and we respond positively and quickly to that invitation demonstrating that progress can be made at pace in our area.

The Finance Director invited a number of her colleagues to suggest ways in which investment in certain changes could lead to greater efficiency. Saira had been waiting for this opportunity for a while and put forward a clear set of propositions that were relevant both for her area and right across the organisation. She had decided that now was the moment to be direct and not coy. She was determined in seeking to set an agenda about changes that could be taken forward across the business. Saira saw this as the moment to lead boldly rather than gradually build a considered consensus.

Reflections
- When is it right to race ahead?
- How do you choose your moment to take a very firm lead on an issue?
- How readily do you accept the need to be taking forward a bold, new approach?

99
Hold your tongue

You may be yearning to say something but know that you need to stay silent.

We have views and want to be influential. We don't want to let the moment pass when we have something to say. We recognise that there are moments when we need to stay quiet and not waste our energy and time shouting out a lot of words. We may feel aggrieved about someone's actions but recognise that expressing immediate criticism could well be counterproductive. We recognise that we need to wait for the right moment to have a conversation rather than blurting out a half thought through, emotional retort.

Saira recognised that she could verbalise her disquiet in a way that was sometimes counterproductive. If a discussion was not going her way, she needed to be alert lest she expressed a defensive response. She needed to think through why others were expressing their particular views and then be clear what end points she wanted to reach. Saira would sometimes tightly press her lips together to signal to her tongue not to burst out into an eloquent, if somewhat, emotive speech.

Reflections
- When might you suffer from verbal diarrhoea?
- What helps you hold back because now is not the most productive moment to express a view?
- When might the words from your tongue be making your emotional reactions even more acute?

100
Chew the fat

Some issues need to be worked through at length before a resolution is reached.

You begin to see a problem as intractable. Your heart sinks whenever you think you need to turn your attention again to addressing that problem. You accept that you need to commit a lot of time to addressing the issue from a range of different perspectives. You try to break the issue down into manageable bites. It feels relentless but you know you have to keep going and engage with a number of people when seeking to take forward the issue constructively.

Saira recognised that her own impatience could get the better of her. She liked operating at speed and wanted to get to quick solutions. Saira recognised that she needed to get the right people in dialogue together to address a seemingly intractable issue thoroughly from a variety of perspectives. Once it was broken down into components with each one being addressed separately, she recognised that progress then became possible.

Reflections
* When has persistence in addressing a difficult issue paid off for you?
* How best do you ensure that you do not give up or let yourself be distracted from handling a seemingly intractable issue?
* How best do you set aside enough time to address difficult issues?

101
Turn over a new leaf

It is time to take a fresh approach and not be contaminated by the past.

We have become relentless in deploying one way of dealing with an issue and have blocked out other perspectives. We have got ourselves into an emotional reaction that has led us to become frustrated, unhappy and aggrieved. We need to make a new start and view issues in a different way. We need to begin to move on from past approaches and decide anew what is the frame of mind that is best suited to achieving what is important.

Saira took a long weekend break after a busy and relentless period. She had got bogged down by the attitudes of some people and knew that some of her reactions had not been helpful. Saira recognised that she needed to re-enter her work after her long weekend with a different frame of mind seeing the positives in what others were contributing. Saira was not sure how easily she would be able to maintain this approach but she was going to give it a try.

Reflections
* How do you recognise when you need to have a fresh start in how you approach an issue?
* When might your emotional reactions be stopping you from bringing a new frame of mind to addressing a persistent issue?
* Who enables you to think anew about how you are going to tackle a difficult issue?

102
Go on all fours

There are times when we need to creep quietly and unobtrusively.

There are moments when it is helpful to approach an issue unobtrusively observing from a discreet angle and seeking not to make your presence obvious. We want to explore an issue from different perspectives and do not want to cause any stir whilst doing so. We do not want to prejudge what is happening while we are absorbing the information we are gleaning. We want to be ready to leap forward when the moment is right but we recognise that stealth and quietness is more important than overt action at particular moments.

Saira sometimes felt that issues were being dealt with at too high a level. She needed to understand more about what employees and clients were thinking before actions were agreed. She wanted quietly but purposefully to engage and listen carefully to a variety of different views. As she formulated her ideas, she was careful not to speak too early for fear of having half thought through ideas. Saira talked quietly and carefully to opinion formers before concluding that she was ready to launch her perspective on appropriate next steps.

Reflections
- When do you need to look at an issue bottom up?
- Whose perspectives do you need to seek from those nearest the action?
- What does it mean for you to move forward with stealth?

103
Take forty winks

A brief rest can refresh the brain and enable it to think clearly going forward.

When we slow our brain down and physically move, we are refreshing our body and allowing our brain to be making connections subconsciously. After seemingly switching off your brain for a few minutes, your next steps can become clearer when you reengage with an issue. The process of a short break of say five minutes can have a noticeable effect in allowing different bits of information to be connected in your brain so that next steps become clearer. Even a five-minute break can have a profound impact especially if associated with some physical movement.

Salra always operated at a fast pace. If she slowed down, she regarded that as a sign of failure and not a justifiable means of looking after herself. After a period of pneumonia, she recognised that she needed to look after herself better. She still wanted to be engaged in demanding work, but had taught herself that short breaks were essential to her equanimity and wellbeing.

Reflections
- What type of short break works best for you?
- How do you ensure that you take regular short breaks?
- How best do you invite the brain to connect different pieces of information and then, in due course, to suggest a way forward?

104
Still small voice of calm

Listening to the inner voice gives new insight and resolve.

In any demanding situation there may well be a voice in your head which is giving you advice. These thoughts may come from past experience or from what respected others might do and think in similar situations. It might be worth asking yourself, 'If I was calm in this situation what would I be thinking and doing?'. It might be worth juxtaposing the questions, 'If was bold, what would I do in this situation?'. Although the two questions begin from different premises, they may well elicit the same answer.

Saira recognised that the dominant emotions in her were ones of resolve, commitment and desire to make a difference. She had taught herself through doing mindfulness exercises and yoga, to take herself into a calmer place where there would be a different inner voice speaking to her. She would deliberately ask herself, 'What is the voice of calm wanting to say to me in this situation?'. This helped her move from dealing with immediate effects into asking questions about longer-term consequences of the actions.

Reflections
- How best do you listen to calming voices in your head?
- How best do you juxtapose voices in your head expressing frustration and those advocating calm?
- When has the voice of calm misled you and held you back from taking necessary action?

105
Absence makes the heart grow fonder

There are times when team members need to disengage for a period in order to become a stronger team.

When we work closely together with others, we can reach a point where we know each other too well. We take each other's strengths for granted and notice rough edges in some of the relationships. Some of the conversations feel repetitive and jar. We can feel overwhelmed by being in each other's presence too much. Perhaps there is a need for time spent doing other things so that when we come back into a team mode, we are ready to appreciate each other's strengths and qualities more fully.

Saira could become irritated with a close colleague who kept challenging her. Saira was glad when a holiday arrived, and she did not have to deal with this person for a couple of weeks. What Saira found surprising was that at the end of a holiday she found herself looking forward to engaging with this colleague. This person challenged her in ways that felt painful, but Saira valued her approach and commitment to their shared endeavour.

Reflections
* When might a period of separation lead to renewed respect?
* Who do we look forward to engaging with when we return into the work context and why?
* How do we balance respect and fondness in our approach to colleagues?

106
Any time means no time

Something that can be done at any time often does not get done.

You want to give your volunteers discretion about when they take forward various activities and believe that their commitment to the cause will mean that they are conscientious and will do what they have committed themselves to do. . At the same time, you recognise that volunteers have lots of different priorities and the promise to do something some time might mean it never gets done. You are philosophic that only a proportion of things will get done while others will never happen.

Saira recognised that if she put some activities in the category of tasks she could do at any time then there was every prospect that they would never happen. Saira did not want to put undue pressure on herself but she knew from her own experience that if a task was not crucial, she needed to seek to allocate a time when she would handle that issue and not let it slip and thereby never appear in her plan for the week. She developed the approach of doing each week a couple of non-priority tasks and then ticking them off her forward list.

Reflections
- When is it helpful to say to yourself that a task can be taken forward at any time?
- To what extent is any time equivalent to virtually never?
- How best do you allocate some time to non-priority tasks?

107
Leave well alone

Sometimes an issue is best viewed from a distance and not tackled.

When might you want to tackle an issue when it could be counterproductive to do so? A course of action has been agreed with clear responsibilities: your involvement could dilute the action when your best interest is served by allowing the process to be completed undisrupted by you. Sometimes an individual might be needing to learn a hard lesson and adjust their way of thinking: they need time to work out their own salvation with an intervention by you not being in anyone's interest.

Saira wanted to rescue a colleague from the consequences of mistakes they had made. . On the other hand, Saira recognised that this individual needed to learn from their missteps and adjust their mindset and approach. They needed space and time to work out alone their next steps without the involvement of Saira. She recognised that she needed to bide her time and then show her support when her colleague had adjusted to the bruising experience and was ready to move forward constructively.

Reflections
- When might you feel too protective of an individual?
- What helps you hold back until the right moment to show support?
- What lessons do you draw from when you are best left alone?

108
He laughs best who laughs last

Watch the risk of celebrating prematurely.

It is right to mark progress and to recognise when intermediate steps have been accomplished but overdoing celebrations at intermediate points can lead to complacency and a lack of alertness about how others are moving forward. There can be a risk of becoming smug about having made faster progress than competitors but then if a degree of complacency creeps in competitors can move ahead faster and leave you trailing behind. What matters is keeping people focused on the end goal while enjoying the intermediate moments.

Saira brought infectious enthusiasm into her team. She would create a buzz of delight in progress made. She had learnt from one unfortunate experience where she celebrated too quickly with a desired outcome then being overturned. Saira knew that she could not allow herself and her team to have the full satisfaction of having completed a project until their proposals had been agreed. The moment when the proposals were submitted was rightly an occasion to mark, but the ultimate achievement was agreement to the proposals and not their submission.

Reflections
- How best do you balance celebrating milestones and keeping up forward momentum?
- How best do you ensure you do not prematurely celebrate success?
- In what ways can you keep alert to progress your competitors are making?

109
A penny saved is a penny gained

We can see an efficiency as a painful loss rather than a valuable gain.

We can see the search for efficiency and savings as retrograde when it is providing a stronger base for future activity. As a coaching business we have gradually reduced our office space and gone virtual. When Covid-19 hit we recognised how prescient we had been and how we are now in a good position to operate as a coaching business going forward without excess overheads. We had become much more flexible and were not worried by overheads.

Saira said to new recruits that she wanted to hear their impressions after two months about where resources could be saved and better directed. Saira combined a strong, supportive, continuous and encouraging leadership approach, alongside a forensic belief in value for money and addressing what could be seen as wasteful activities. She was deliberate in seeking to communicate clearly where resources had been diverted to good effect, giving credit to those who had been advocates of such approaches.

Reflections
- How relentless do you need to be on using resources effectively?
- What can you fund going forward through trade-offs from saving resources?
- Is our natural approach to save to spend, or to spend to save?

110
No pain no gain

Making progress inevitably involves a degree of pain.

The pain of hard, physical effort is a precursor to sporting success. The pain of hard intellectual effort is a starting point for finding solutions to difficult problems. Effective challenge can be painful and yet lead to purposeful dialogue and sound conclusions. Pain and progress are interwoven in a way which can feel like hard work. What matters is holding onto the overall intent and recognising that painful exploration is more likely to lead to progress than complacent indifference.

Saira knew that she needed to restructure her team in order to help it move forward. Saira knew that she had to be very clear in the way she communicated the reasons for the changes and how best she was going to support her people through the transition. She wanted to help individuals to develop have their own rationales about the greater good even if their jobs were being radically changed or were disappearing. Saira helped her team recognise that there were possible benefits for them if they moved on into other roles.

Reflections
- When has pain led to better outcomes for you?
- How best do you communicate at a time of pain to keep people as positive as possible?
- How best do you empathize with people's pain while keeping a clear focus on what is best for the organisation?

111
Still waters run deep

If someone is quiet don't underestimate what they are able to offer.

The views of quiet members of a team may be at risk of being ignored when their contribution will be equally of value and perhaps more significant. The reflective person can often link points together and see longer-term consequences than those who are operating in the moment and being instinctive in their reactions. A key skill of any chair is to draw in those who are quieter, recognising that they often bring a valuable depth of understanding and perspective.

Saira recruited a colleague with whom she had worked before who she knew who would always give, quiet, thoughtful advice. He was good at absorbing information and distilling it down to key points. Saira knew that any conversation with this colleague would calm her and provide her with valuable insights. There was a stillness and quietness in this colleague that rubbed off on Saira when she was relentlessly focused on individual issues. Saira made sure that this individual was never underestimated by other members of the team.

Reflections
- When are you at risk of writing off quiet people?
- How do you draw the best out of those around you who are relatively quiet?
- How do you ensure there is enough space given to the quieter people in any discussion?

112
Beware going into overdrive

There are times when our speed needs to be fast but we need to watch becoming exhausted.

You know that you can move into a deliberate, quick thinking and decisive operating mode when this needed. You enjoy the buzz that flows from being part of fast-moving situations where you can make a useful contribution. You enjoy the camaraderie and that sense of fulfilment, but at the same time, you recognise that it can exhaust you. You know that you need to be cognisant of the risks and build in time when you can be operating at a slower pace. You need space at a weekend more than ever before.

When Saira was at risk of going into overdrive the best antidote was to spend time with her children which helped put the rest of life into a different perspective. Sometimes what was needed was all-consuming activity with her children to counteract the activity of work. On other occasions what was most valuable was quiet reflective space with her children, reading to them or watching children's programs with them.

Reflections
- Be alert to when you might go into overdrive
- Recognise the times when overdrive can lead to anxiety and exhaustion
- Seek to time limit overdrive deliberately and to scope weekends at a slower pace to complement the overdrive you are deploying at work

113
Watch the chip on the shoulder

Be mindful about what you can cause you to be resentful and don't let it cloud your judgement.

A thoughtful boss asked me early in my career if there was a risk that I had a chip on my shoulder about not having gone to a well-known school or to Oxbridge. Their comment was the wake-up call that I needed to think and move forward based on who I was and what my background was and not consider that my education was inferior to others. Coaching conversations often involve helping individuals reframe their background and experience from one of apology into one of celebrating and drawing fully on their unique background. Their background then becomes a source of perspective and not a distorting lens.

Saira felt that she had been to a third-rate university and kept seeking to demonstrate that she could operate at the same level of effectiveness as those who had supposedly had a better education. The universal acclamation she received from successive bosses gradually reduced this distorted self-image, but this feeling of inferiority would periodically appear and needed to be recognised and diluted.

Reflections
- What might be your underlying resentments?
- How have those resentments given you a sense of energy and purpose?
- How can you counter any exhausting sense of resentment or inferiority that is inhibiting your progress?

114
Watch if your heart is in your boots

When we are consistently glum, we undermine our prospect of making progress.

A sense of hope and expectancy can drive us forward. We hold the prospect of better times ahead which keep us motivated, but our joy can sink a long way when we feel stalled. The enjoyment in our work disappears and we feel that any sense of fun in our work has gone. We need something to raise our spirits and help us see that there are possibilities ahead. We look for encouragement from others but sense that progress is going to be slow. We recognise that we have to trudge on one step at a time.

Saira recognised that if her children were unhappy and her work was not fulfilling that her enjoyment in life would feel squeezed. She needed something to keep her cheerful when life was tough which might be talking to friends who encouraged her or having a conversation with her coach. She recognised that her lowness could be infectious and hence, she needed to seek to catch low periods at an early stage.

Reflections
- What warning signs do you get that you are going to feel low?
- What patterns do you observe in how you can move through a period of being low?
- How do you reduce the detrimental effect on others of a low period?

115
Keep your distance

Be mindful if you get too aligned with some colleagues and thereby at risk of being blinkered in your approach.

In good teams you build a closeness with colleagues and yet need to keep a distance to remain objective in assessing which working relationships are being productive. Getting too close to someone can mean that you absorb their prejudices and mirror their behaviours in ways that might be unhelpful. In any work context it can be worth asking yourself, 'how best do I keep a sensible distance in order to remain objective about what is happening?'.

Saira felt alignment with a trusted colleague but recognised it was important to maintain a strong degree of independence in her thinking and her contribution in order to be fully effective. Her partnership with her colleague was mutually supportive but there were moments when the two of them needed to bring out their own distinctive contribution. If they always agreed they would be regarded as being in cahoots and, therefore, taken less seriously.

Reflections
- When might you be too close to someone for your own good?
- How best do you maintain a strong sense of mutual support alongside effective challenge?
- When might you be at risk of distancing yourself too much from your colleagues?

116
A cat has nine lives

One mishap or apparent failure does not necessarily have terminal consequences.

We might be fearful that after one misstep our career will be blighted for ever. We are apprehensive about saying or doing the wrong thing for fear that our reputation is tarnished and we will never be able to recover. We suspect that a failure may haunt us for the rest of our lives if we make a mistake. We observe others who seem to keep recovering from major mishaps: perhaps we can take reassurance from their experience and recognise that you can recover from misadventures and learn more from failures than apparent successes.

Saira was for ever getting into situations when her suggestions did not quite work as well as she had hoped, or when she became at cross purposes with influential people. She was adaptable enough to recover from situations which others would have found devastating. When something went wrong and her reputation was at stake, she was able to demonstrate how she was making progress in other areas. Her speed of response got her into tricky situations enabled her to rebuild her reputation quickly.

Reflections
- How best do you move on from painful situations?
- How do you balance apparent failure with forward progress?
- When do you need to use feline cunning?

117
An idle brain is the Devil's workshop

When we are not busy might we get into mischief?

When we are less busy it is an opportunity to develop our learning or thinking in new areas or to catch up on lower priority tasks, but when the pressure is off there can be a tendency to mull over issues in ways that are counterproductive. We might keep reviewing something that went wrong when we did not make the impact we had hoped and dwell on the behaviours of others which we consider inept or underhand. When we are less busy, we can begin to dwell on fears that are unreal or become preoccupied by thinking how we might manipulate a situation to suit our ends.

Saira recognised that if she had too much time on her hands, she could see plots where none existed. If she had lots of time to think about someone's motives, she would tend to dwell on the negative risks rather than the positive opportunities.

Reflections
- When you are idle how do you ensure you focus more on opportunities and not threats?
- When are you at risk of seeing manipulative behaviours which distort the reality of what is happening?
- How best do you spot when you might want to manipulate a situation in your favour?

118
An ounce of protection is worth a pound of cure

Prevention can be a better investment than spending on recovery.

Every organisation focusing on the public's health believes that investment in health protection saves significantly more money on healthcare expenditure over the longer term. We protect our children to minimise the risks of physical accidents or emotional trauma. When a project is going wrong, we seek to protect the elements that are working while seeking to address underlying issues. Protection might seem at first to be a negative concept, but good endeavours start off by wanting to nurture what is good which can be built on for the future.

Saira was told that part of her enterprise was not delivering in a way the bosses wanted with fundamental issues needing to be addressed. Saira recognised the issues: her starting point was to look at what was working well in the organisation and to preserve good characteristics while making fundamental changes. There were elements she wanted to nurture and protect so that they could flourish amidst an organisation which was needing radical overhaul.

Reflections
- How best do you protect the good and not be over protective of the indifferent?
- What enables you to see the good that can be built on in any situation where a fundamental rethink is needed?
- When might you be over protective in a way that is counterproductive?

119
A task begun is half done

Once we get started, we are halfway to achieving our goal.

Often the biggest hurdle is the shaping of a project or task. We want to be clear how the components fit together and what is the destination and the end goal. When we feel no sense of forward momentum and are still working through how to tackle an issue, we can become low and defeatist. As soon as we have a plan and have taken the first step, we are on course to reach our destination, even though we might have taken only limited progress so far.

Saira was dependent on decisions by a key committee. Once this group had agreed on a particular program, she knew she would have the authority to take the program through to completion. Key was the initial presentation committee seeking endorsement. Once that backing had been agreed, and the task begun, Saira knew that she was set well for delivering the outcomes.

Reflections
* When do you recognise that a task or program has properly begin?
* Can you allow yourself to believe that when a project has properly started, that it is well on the way to delivery?
* What enables you to move from ideas to getting a task started?

120
Beauty is only skin deep

Don't be taken in by appearances.

We can feel overawed by something that looks perfect. We do not believe that we can produce a product or outcome of the same quality. We observe someone as a potential ideal recruit and don't necessarily explore their background fully to understand some of their foibles. Everyone has quirks. It is helpful to admire qualities in people and situations while recognising that there will be tensions and imperfections. It is only as imperfections are recognised that there can be realistic progress.

Saira recognised that the contractors she was talking with were all seeking to offer a perfect product. She probed them about how they would respond to unpredictable events and how they would recover when their timetable was thrown into doubt. She pushed them hard about their resilience and responsiveness knowing that as soon as the project began that there would be inevitable problems. Saira appreciated the neatness with which contractors put together their plans but recognised that glossy presentations could mean that the contractor was more concerned with the superficial than sustainable consequences.

Reflections
* When are you at risk of being taken in by appearances of perfection?
* How do you assess what is the substantive offering when presentations are slick?
* How do you build an understanding that what matters most is substance rather than presentation?

121
Better to wear out than rust out

It is better to keep active and engaged rather than isolated and impotent.

At any age keeping active and engaged is important for mental alertness, physical fitness and emotional wellbeing. When we keep our brain active and our hearts sensitive to the needs of others, we can be responsive to the world around us and adaptable to different situations and needs. If we stay still our minds can fossilize, our physique can deteriorate and our emotions can become insensitive and warped by isolation. We stand the risk of becoming frozen in time and not able to slot in effectively with potential companions and collaborators.

Saira was balancing regularly her need for movement and stillness. She thrived by seeking to keep mentally, spiritually, physically, and emotionally alert and active. She also knew that stillness and moments of reflection were important to you. She did not want to stay still for too long for fear of becoming too set in her ways or stale. Perhaps she veered too much on the need to keep perpetually active, but she recognised that this was the best way of her maintaining her equilibrium and wellbeing.

Reflections
- What keeps you active and agile, physically and intellectually, spiritually and emotionally?
- When might you be at risk of wearing yourself out?
- When might some perceptions begin to ossify?

122
Cross the stream where it is at its shallowest

Be practical and don't make things difficult for yourself.

There can be moments of bravado when we want to demonstrate to ourselves and others that we can do difficult things well. There is a time to take the adventurous path and demonstrate to ourselves and others that outcomes can be achieved in ways that had not previously been expected. It is helpful to reflect on what is the simplest and direct way to reach an outcome. We can overcomplicate the steps needed when a helpful question is, 'how do we get from here to our destination as simply and cleanly as possible?'.

Saira would sometimes ask the question, 'if we were to get from A to B in two stages what would they be?'. Her technique was to prompt people to focus on the simplest and most straightforward way of addressing an issue. She recognised that it would then be right to explore the complications, but she wanted to start with a straightforward proposition and then examine what the complications and risks might be.

Reflections
- What can get in the way of seeing the straightforward solution?
- When are you at risk of hankering for a complicated solution?
- How useful is it to ask what are the two key steps needed to reach an outcome?

123
Laugh and the world laughs with you

A smile is infectious and a growl is contagious.

There is a natural reaction to mirror the behaviour of others. When we smile others are more likely to smile too. When we look grumpy others are much more likely to respond in a grumpy fashion. Bringing humour into a meeting to enable people to see the funny side of things can defuse tense meetings and allow people to become more positive in their engagement. If a meeting can end on a lighter note with participants leaving smiling, they are much more likely to remember the meeting as enjoyable rather than painful. Laughing at situations can bring a lightness to a conversation. Laughing at people creates an apprehension that I might also be about to be laughed at.

Saira brought a cheerful demeanour and could readily make people smile. She knew that if people enjoyed working with her, they were much more likely to respond to her requests. She was always looking for the humorous in any situation and was willing to gently tease others and happy to be teased herself. She built a sense of camaraderie enabling people to laugh together.

Reflections
- How infectious is your smile?
- How do you use humour in a way that lightens a conversation?
- How do you bring joy to complicated meetings?

124
Bottle the positives

It provides a good basis for the future if the positives in difficult situations can be captured.

One organisation coming through the Covid-19 crisis talked of 'bottling the positives'. This metaphor provided a good way of capturing the positive changes that flowed from home working and the need to respond quickly to changing circumstances. Barriers had been broken down and new ways of working had been introduced quickly with a far better use of digital opportunities. There was a risk that people reverted to previous ways of working after the lock-down ended, hence the desire to identify breakthroughs in ways of delivering work and working together that would be valuable over the longer-term.

Saira had previously felt slightly guilty about spending one day a week working at home. In the period when a lot of people were working at home it became much more the accepted norm. Saira felt there had been a breakthrough in respect for people working at home. She wanted to ensure that ways of working in the future allowed a balance between working virtually and working in the same physical space as colleagues.

Reflections
- How best do you look for positives in a crisis?
- How best do you capture and hold onto positive changes in working practices?
- What underlying values do you want to ensure are not lost when an organisation moves on after disruptions?

Risks to watch: beware lest you…

125
Turn up your nose

Beware lest your body language implies disapproval or disdain.

You are working hard to achieve an outcome and you receive a comment that seems unhelpful. You feel irritation and do not think the observation is well founded. You know you have to take account of the comment and be patient, but your whole body feels a sense of annoyance and your facial expression gives away the fact that you want to dismiss the comment as irrelevant, unhelpful or just wrong. You signal your reaction through your body language before you have thought through how best to respond constructively to the observations.

Harry recognised that he could sometimes look dismissive. His colleagues knew from his physical reaction what words he would then say. There could be a disapproving tone in both his actions and his words. He sought to engage brain then mouth then body in that order, but too often it was body, mouth and then brain. Harry needed trusted others to tell him when hints of disapproval were beginning to show in his demeanour.

Reflections
- When do your physical expressions give away your frame of mind?
- How best do you keep a neutral facial expression when you are thinking something through you are going to react?
- When might it be helpful to give an early signal of disapproval?

126
Live from hand to mouth

Beware lest you only focus on the present and don't prepare for the future.

Sometimes we have to live in the present and not be too concerned about the future. There may be a welter of things to do and we have to get the immediate done, but there is always the opportunity to begin to look ahead and capture the learning from what has been happening. When we continue to live in the present, we can be caught out by people who are thinking into future opportunities and we become left behind. We think we have been doing the right things by focusing on the immediate without seeing some of the consequences which we should have addressed but had not found the time to do so.

Harry loved dealing with immediate problems. He got a lot of satisfaction in ticking lines off his 'to do' list and pointing to where he had won people's support. As a politician he knew that as well as winning people's approval in the short-term he needed to be advocating a future direction. He needed to build credibility as someone setting a coherent, forward direction and not just as a solver of immediate problems.

Reflections
- When is it right to be purely concerned with the immediate?
- What is stopping you focusing more on longer-term considerations?
- How best do you prepare for your own future?

127
Act the goat

Beware lest you behave in ways that others regard as foolish.

We may want to be rebellious and show that the status quo is not sustainable. We seek to bring measured and constructive arguments drawing on evidence we regard as irrefutable. We don't seem to be making progress and we resort to the extravagant and the eye-catching. We then feel that we are making progress with some people engaging with us, but we wonder whether they are viewing us as outlandish and ill-considered. We recognise that we need to revert to putting forward a rational, well-argued case once we have caught people's attention.

Harry would sometimes tell a far-fetched story in order to catch people's attention. He was prepared to risk looking foolish in order for people to be engaging with what he was saying. Having caught people's attention he would then hone in on key points that he considered important and use nuggets of evidence to illustrate a way forward. Harry did recognise that he could overdo this tendency to be outlandish and a touch oafish.

Reflections
- Recognise when you might be overdoing comments that might be regarded as absurd or foolish.
- Know how you grab people's attention without tarnishing your reputation.
- Accept that being willing to make yourself look slightly foolish in a good cause can build up a degree of affection.

128
Ride the high horse

Beware lest you appear to regard as irrelevant good points made by others.

The strong horse pounding through a field is squashing the undergrowth with no-one wanting to come near to the horse for fear of being hurt. Sometimes we may be using our position to assert in a dogmatic way a particular way forward. We believe clear direction is needed and expect people to follow because of the strength of our argument. We risk being insensitive to people who feel their views are being squashed. They keep out of our way because they do not want to feel trampled on by the force of our rhetoric.

Harry recognised that he enjoyed telling people what they ought to think. He had admired a local Free Church preacher in his youth and had adopted some of their techniques in his speeches as a politician. He knew that sometimes he had to speak above hecklers and, therefore, had developed a rather dogmatic and sometimes shrill tone. Harry also recognised the dangers in his approach of appearing overzealous and dogmatic and not appearing to listen to those people whose votes he needed.

Reflections
- When might you overstate your arguments?
- When might you come over as shrill and unempathetic?
- How best do you judge when to soften your tone?

129
Play with fire

Be mindful of the potential consequences if you enter controversial territory.

There are some topics for most groups or teams which can feel very controversial. When you enter that space, you are conscious that your comments are being observed very carefully. A hush can descend as you raise an issue that has been controversial, especially if you suggest a way forward that might produce an emotional reaction. When a controversial issue needs to be considered, preparing the way is crucial so that participants are willing to address an issue as rationally as possible without being clouded by deep-seated, emotional reactions.

Harry was conscious that in his local political party some divisive issues were hardly ever spoken about. Harry recognised that he would undermine his support if he set out views that were not aligned with local members. Harry recognised that he had to be pragmatic in reconciling his own political beliefs with the preferences within his local party. But there were times when he felt he had no choice other than to set out why he disagreed with the local party, recognising that this might put his own future at risk.

Reflections
- When do you avoid entering controversial territory?
- When do you choose your moment to make a proposition that will inevitably lead to disagreement?
- When is it helpful to say something controversial?

130
Let the cat out of the bag

Be mindful if you share thinking before it has been properly developed.

When we know a piece of information it is quite difficult to imagine not knowing that piece of information, and be able to respond to questions in a neutral way. When an idea is being developed it can be counterproductive for a hint of that possibility to be shared before the idea is set out in a more complete way. We need to keep reminding ourselves that we know more than we might realise and that how we describe something will draw on our full knowledge.

Harry enjoyed his interaction with journalists but was always wary. Sometimes he would be deliberate in sharing an idea with a journalist recognising that the information would feed into a newspaper story. On other occasions Harry tried hard to un-remember something so that he did not imply likely next steps although he knew what was intended. Harry did not want to be disingenuous but recognised that it would be counterproductive to share information before it had been fully developed.

Reflections
* When are you at risk of inadvertently sharing information told to you in confidence?
* What techniques work for you in terms of blanking out private information?
* In what situations do you need to be doubly careful that an inadvertent comment from you is counterproductive?

131
Rush from pillar to post

Beware lest you jump from one possibility to another without thinking through your actions.

When life feels frenetic, we rush from one task to another. Our sense of achievement can flow from crossing off items on the 'to do' list or squeezing in as many meetings as we can into a day. We might quite enjoy intense activity and making small bits of progress, but it can feel rushed, frantic and never-ending. We have to force ourselves to stop and take a break. We have to prioritise and recognise that good enough is going to be good enough and need to recognise that some things are not going to get done if there is to be time allocated to look beyond the immediate tasks.

Harry was being harangued by a relentless sequence of e-mails which he felt obliged to answer. One minute a concern was refuse collection, and then education, immediately followed by problems at a particular hospital. He felt pushed around relentlessly, unable to prioritise. He knew he needed to set aside enough time for the immediate and have protected time for the important and longer term.

Reflection
- When are you at risk of not stopping?
- How do you stop bouncing from one immediate issue to another?
- How do you seek to set aside time for the important and longer-term?

132
Create a storm in a teacup

Be mindful when you might stir up a dispute on a minor issue which absorbs attention that should have gone onto bigger issues.

You will probably have observed occasions when someone stirs up controversy on a small issue attracting a lot of attention from the people who otherwise would have been dealing with more important matters. You observe someone being so preoccupied with one issue that they did not let go when it was clear this was not the moment to try and create a different way forward. You want to be more mindful about when you stir up an issue recognising how your intervention is going to be received.

Harry sometimes deliberately expressed controversial views on local issues. Sometimes this approach was helpful and on other occasions it led to criticism that he was too preoccupied with minor issues and not focusing on the fundamental issues affecting the area he represented. He recognised that he could only generate a certain amount of press interest and over time became more deliberate about the issues he stirred.

Reflection
- When do you deliberately want to stir up an issue and how do you do it?
- What did you learn from others who have created a localised storm in terms of what worked or didn't work?
- How do you stop yourself from creating an unnecessary storm?

133
Are the fly in the ointment

Recognise when you can be disrupting a potentially good outcome.

We may want to advocate a particular perspective in a determined way. We recognise that others are building a consensus around a different approach. We don't want to disrupt this development of a shared view about priorities going forward, but we do think that ignoring our perspective is disrespectful and potentially myopic. We ask ourselves what is the greater good: is it a unified approach that does not take account of our points but is still going to be reasonably effective, or do we keep banging away advocating our perspective which is not getting any traction?

Harry liked being a rebel. He wanted to be different to his colleague politicians, but he became very sensitive if his political opponents tried to drive a wedge between him and his fellow party members. He wanted to be both aligned with his colleagues and able to express contrary views persuasively. Harry and his party colleagues came to accept that there were going to be moments when he expressed different views. Nonetheless, they accepted him as a valued member of their political grouping.

Reflection
* Be deliberate when you decide to go with the majority view?
* Be considered and measured when expressing views contrary to an emerging consensus?
* Accept that sometimes you will feel isolated and needing to withdraw your objections?

134
Clutch at straws

Beware holding tightly onto minor or unsubstantiated evidence in support of your viewpoint.

You may remember a situation where you were beginning to lose an argument and kept repeating pieces of information that you described as key. You recognise it would have been better to stop arguing and gracefully withdraw, either accepting that you were not going to win the argument or regrouping to return with a stronger evidence base. You recognise there is a danger that when you feel forced into a corner that you cling onto perspectives and assumptions that may have become outdated.

Harry recognised that he could sometimes hold onto assumptions for too long. He accepted that he wasn't always flexible in his thinking relying too much relied on some 'killer' facts. He knew that he had to restock his evidence base on a regular basis and be watchful if he built an approach to a problem based purely on a couple of examples. He needed to keep testing his thinking to ensure that his points could be justified by a wider body of evidence.

Reflections
* When might you place too much reliance on one or two key facts?
* How open are you to new information which is contrary to facts you have previously held dear?
* When might you decide to think afresh about an issue and look for a new set of indicators?

135
Are left high and dry

Beware lest you become isolated without an obvious way forward.

You are advocating a particular way forward and think you have substantial support. You are a little surprised that your colleagues are not more vocal in supporting you, but you assume that there is a shared, common interest which will mean that your view is going to prevail. You begin to realise that the support for your proposition has gradually ebbed away. When you speak up nobody comes in to support your proposition. You are slightly disappointed in yourself for not realising that you were likely to become isolated and a lone voice.

Harry recognised that his public statements were met either with a lot of support or were quietly ignored. When he committed himself to supporting a particular cause he recognised that he needed to keep a careful eye on whether that cause continued to be recognised as important. On too many occasions he had found that he kept backing a proposal that had lost favour with him at risk of being seen as out-dated and out of touch.

Reflections
* When might your supporters desert you?
* How best do you keep in touch with those people whose support you need?
* When are you fine about being isolated and a lone voice?

Nurture a pet lamb who becomes a cross ram

Beware if you over protect someone who then becomes frustrated and potentially destructive.

You want to be helpful and nurture people who are struggling. You give them a lot of attention, but might be at risk of over protecting them rather than letting them learn through their bruising experiences. You remember when you over protected someone who then did not develop the ability to handle disagreement and conflict. They did not learn how to rub along with people who were more pushy than them: as a consequence, they became disillusioned and frustrated. They reached a point when they resented the fact that they had been protected from the rough and tumble of organisational life and became either over sensitive or obtuse, and difficult to manage.

Harry was keen on selecting young, able people to support him. He tutored them but then expected them to handle difficult meetings capably without too much protection from him. Harry knew that these young people, in order to grow into effective advocates, needed to develop resilience that would keep them balanced and proportionate whatever situation they were facing.

Reflections
- Enjoy nurturing young talent but don't over protect.
- Be mindful if you are stopping people from learning when they need to go through difficult scrapes.
- Enjoy releasing people so that they are no longer in your shadow.

137
Grasp all and lose all

Be mindful if you seek to grip an outcome or option too early before all the considerations are clear.

You want to push to a conclusion. An initial outcome looks attractive and you think will satisfy your requirements. You seek to close down a conversation quickly because you have seen a way forward. In all these examples a bit more patience could have been helpful to hear more people's views and to test out different scenarios a bit more fully. Starting with an understanding of where you want to be at the end of an exercise can help inform how early decisions are made.

Harry recognised that in his impatience he could seek to reach conclusions in conversations prematurely. He had to keep reminding himself to wait until people had begun to accept a way forward. If he tried to close down a conversation too quickly and assume agreement, he would risk not having the full agreement of others. He needed to judge when, through exhaustion or through having worked through the options, his colleagues were ready to endorse a preferred approach.

Reflections
- How best do you hold back when you want to grip an opportunity quickly?
- How might you reach agreement in small steps rather than relying on one big agreement?
- What helps you recognise what you will lose if you seek to crystallize a conclusion too quickly?

138
Run into a brick wall

Be observant and realistic about obstacles that are not going to be overcome.

We have all observed people bringing being unrealistic and not recognising that a barrier is insurmountable. If there is no money available continually pressing for further funding is dispiriting and a waste of time. A good leader will be assessing where they have a prospect of pressing a case successfully and when the answer is inevitably going to be no. Any barrier needs to be viewed carefully to see what might be the options of going round or over it. Sometimes a barrier has to be accepted as a fixed point, at least for the foreseeable future.

Harry wanted to change his Party's policy in a particular area and articulated what he thought was a persuasive argument, but there were deeply intrenched views that meant his approach was getting little traction. He wanted to be persistent in arguing his case, but had to remind himself that this would be a waste of time and energy for the immediate future. But one day people might move on or become more open to fresh thinking..

Reflections
* How best do you determine whether a barrier is immovable or insurmountable?
* What helps you look ahead to see significant impediments before you?
* What helps you slow down and view objectively potential blockers?

139
Flog a dead horse

Beware lest you repeatedly argue the same point and receive an increasingly negative response.

I have observed people feeling so passionately about a particular point that they relentlessly make the same observation. Their colleagues become increasingly frustrated by the individual's repetitive intervention. When you are losing an argument, it is better to withdraw and regroup and accept the conclusion of the majority, or reframe your point in the light of new evidence and choose a different moment to advocate the course of action which you think is right.

Harry could be persistent in making a point on a number of occasions with different pieces of evidence to support what he was advocating. He could use humour well to keep people's interest, but there was a point where he knew he had to stop and withdraw. He would remind himself to assess the probabilities of success so he did not waste his time on lost causes. He needed to be open to modifying his preferred approach.

Reflections
- How best do you assess whether you are winning people over to your point of views?
- What is the risk that your pride does not let you withdraw?
- How readily do you recognise when you are saying something for the sake of it rather than because you believe in it?

140
Slide down a slippery slope

Beware lest you slip into a position that is not easily defended.

You concede that people can leave work half an hour early on a Friday. A subsequent momentum builds up with staff wanting to leave one hour early on a Friday. You had built in a concession that people wanted to push further. On another occasion you decide not to question someone's behaviour that is bordering on the bullying: a few weeks' later you get feedback that this individual has been putting unreasonable demands on some individuals. You recognise you have given an opening to changes in accepted behaviours that you are now regretting.

Harry tried to be disciplined in replying to correspondence. When he was tired, he told himself that some correspondence had to wait: he began to get used to not replying to correspondence as quickly as he had previously wanted to do. His secretary pointed out to him that he was letting his standards slip. Harry was grumpy with this observation at first, but recognised that he had been gradually reducing the importance he attached to responding to members of the public.

Reflections
- When might you have let your standards slip?
- How bothered are you about being consistent in the way you deal with priorities and people?
- What helps you to maintain standards that are important to you in particular areas?

141
Be alert to when you have cold feet

Be mindful why you are losing interest in taking a particular course of action.

You felt strongly that a particular approach is correct and built arguments in support of a particular route. You notice that your enthusiasm has got less for this course of action and don't fully understand why you are feeling more hesitant. Being hesitant about a course of action gives us useful data to then consider whether this hesitancy is for good, sound, logical reasons or whether there is an emotional concern to avoid potential, adverse comment that we would find painful.

Harry was good at judging how much support he would receive for a particular approach. Sometimes though there was a strong emotional reaction which was inhibiting him from taking a particular approach. This was sometimes expressed in a physical response of becoming hot or sweating. He recognised that the root of the problem was going to be an emotional reaction to being rejected by people whose support he valued. He recognised that he needed in these situations to let the rational trump the emotional and not be over sensitive to criticism from others.

Reflections
- Be mindful when your enthusiasm for a way forward dissipates?
- Observe what your body is telling you about dangers in a particular situation?
- Seek to identify why your hesitancy has kicked in?

142
Expect everything to be copper-bottomed

Beware if you think your favoured option will be fully supported by all the evidence.

In a crisis, decisions have to be made on the basis of whatever evidence is available. You think through what the evidence is telling you and what the pros and cons are of different courses of action. There are so many imponderables that no favoured solution is going to be the perfect answer because the data does not lead to one approach. Where decisions are made at speed you have to rely on partial and not complete information.

Harry used to get cross if the figures kept changing. He got resentful if his favoured option was refuted because someone else had data which pointed in a different direction to his preferred course of action. Harry knew from his time working in a charity that decisions had to be based on partial information and kept telling himself that his job was to recognise the links between different pieces of information and make the best judgement that he could in the circumstances.

Reflections
* Beware lest you are seeking perfection before you decide on a course of action?
* Be deliberate in saying what are the key pieces of information that will shape your thinking?
* Seek to influence people's expectations about what data or analysis can realistically be available?

143
Are a wet blanket

Beware lest you are continually dampening people's motivation to solve a problem.

Every team needs someone who can identify the downsides of a proposed course of action and ask difficult questions. Those people who do this well have contracted with their colleagues so that they recognise that their drawing attention to unexpected consequences is a valuable part of working through issues and next steps. There is a skill in putting negative and challenging points in a way which respects the goal that is being sought and the efforts that are being put into the enterprise.

Harry knew that some people regarded him as grumpy and negative. He could see all too quickly what ideas were going to fall flat. He recognised that he more readily saw problems than solutions. He tried to ensure that when his comments were likely to be regarded as unhelpful that he explained his reasons for his views, while fully respecting the hard work that had been put into addressing the issue. He wanted to leave people thinking their efforts were worthwhile even if the right solution had not yet been identified.

Reflections
- When might you be putting a dampener on peoples' ideas without realising you are doing it?
- How do you express both caution and enthusiasm at the same time?
- How best do you balance bringing challenge and praise within the same conversation?

144
Get carried away with excitement

Beware if your enthusiasms go beyond the evidence.

We can be thrilled about initial successes and believe that if we keep going in a particular direction that we will create unprecedented success. We are full of excitement and enthusiasm and believe nothing can get in our way. The risk is that because of our excitement we are not alert to danger signs and we think that the momentum is shared by more people than is the case in reality.

Harry was passionate about the importance of advocating educational opportunities for those aged over sixty. He saw this as a way of keeping people healthy and interested in life, but others in his political grouping were less committed to this priority. They used words of support but when it came to advocating how local government spent its resources, the priority of his political colleagues was for school education. Harry did not want to let go of this enthusiasm for education for those over sixty while recognising that he would lose some goodwill from younger members of his party.

Reflections
- What is exciting you about the opportunities currently before you?
- How securely based on facts are those excitements?
- How can you use the energy generated by excitement to enable you to deliver the progress you particularly want to see happen?

145
Are viewed as being as blind as a bat

Beware if you develop the reputation of not being able to see the obvious.

You are being single-minded in pursuit of a particular objective and do not see or you blank out views or factors that are not aligned with your preferred direction of travel. This approach gives you a sense of purpose but carries the risk of not seeing the risks or not being alert to the implications of new data or unforeseen events. Others can begin to see an emerging problem, but you are viewed as relentlessly keeping your attention focused on your personal or previously agreed objectives.

Harry knew that he could sometimes be too single-minded for his own good. He was resolute in striving to persuade people in favour of supporting particular outcomes. His determination was a great asset and a risk. He did not always spot impending trouble or take account of how trends were changing which would put at risk what he was seeking to achieve. He knew that he needed trusted advisors alongside him who would be his eyes and ears to alert him to impending issues.

Reflections
- When might you be too blinkered for your own good?
- What do you not want to see and, therefore, do not look out for?
- Who are your 'eyes and ears'?

146
Are seen as a peppery individual

Beware lest you bring more discord into an engagement than is helpful.

Some conversations can seem bland with limited progress. You want to shake things up and contribute a perspective that is contrary to the accepted trends or a question that seeks to change the direction of a conversation. You want to hype up a debate so there is more energy. You want to put a bit of heat into the dialogue so that people take their thinking in a new direction and go out of their individual comfort zones. You want to provoke with a purpose, while being sensitive to how your interjections will land. Done deliberately, this approach can be a powerful stimulus. Overdone, it can lead to discord.

Harry enjoyed interjecting with provocative questions. He knew this was both a strength and a liability if overdone. It was a plus when people were ready for good quality debate, but could have the consequence that some people were sometimes more hesitant to contribute because they felt that there was a degree of unpredictability in Harry's contributions.

Reflections
- When do you want to spice up a meeting because it is too bland?
- How best do you ask a provocative question in a way that leads to good dialogue rather than discord?
- When do you need to temper your desire to be provocative in a meeting?

147
Are always sat on the fence

Beware lest you are viewed as someone who will continually equivocate.

Sitting on a sturdy fence can give you a chance to look at the different elements in the landscape. Sitting on a barbed wire fence will be distracting and painful. There are moments to survey a scene and consider which route to take going forward. There is an expectation on all leaders to make decisions in a timely way. Constant procrastination undermines respect for a leader as quickly as does ill-judged decisions.

Harry was being pressed by his colleagues to support a particular proposal. Harry wanted time to talk with a number of people but recognised that he could not procrastinate for too long. He said he would decide on his view within ten days and used that time to talk deliberately to a number of influential people. After the ten days Harry recognised that he needed to express a view. His credibility depended on having been seen to weigh up the issues and express a considered view.

Reflections
- When is it helpful to say you are not ready to express a definitive view?
- When might it be helpful to say you will express a view in a specified number of days' time?
- How best do you assess how much irritation you are causing others through your procrastination?

148
Are seen as playing fast and loose

Beware lest you are seen as behaving irresponsibly and taking advantage of a situation with no regard to previous commitment.

You thought you had built mutual understanding with a colleague about next steps on a particular proposal. You get feedback that your colleague is giving a slightly different message to others and putting himself in the lead rather than it being a joint endeavour. You are not sure whether what you are hearing is an accurate or distorted narrative. You choose a moment to talk openly with your colleague about your concerns and conclude that you are aligned and that the message you received was not accurate.

Harry had a quick mind and was seeing opportunities develop. As he saw the context change, he evolved his narrative in describing the rationale for a particular approach. He had to be careful that he was consistent in communicating with his colleagues, why his perspective was evolving. Harry knew that maintaining trust was key and that he should keep his colleagues fully informed of what he was communicating to avoid misrepresentation.

Reflections
- When might you be at risk of racing ahead of others and risk losing their trust?
- How best do you ensure that acting quickly does not look as if you are acting irresponsibly?
- When do you need to deliberately hold back to let others catch up with you?

149
Get into hot water

Be mindful when you are beginning to cause discord.

Those around us have expectations of what we will do and how we will engage with them. We assume their goodwill and take forward ideas believing that others will automatically endorse whatever we say and do. We can be at risk of assuming support and patronage whatever we do and may not recognise that we can inadvertently create discord because we have moved on from our previous approach. We may not realise there is a problem until faced with the views of unhappy people.

Harry was often getting himself into situations of minor conflict with his colleagues. He was full of ideas and kept wanting to develop proposals in the light of the myriad of conversations he was having with local people. He recognised that he could go too quickly into critical observations, saying or writing things that others viewed as unwarranted or not based on previous agreements. Harry kept trying to hold himself back but was not always successful.

Reflections
- How best do you assess how your comments are going to land with your colleagues?
- How much do you care if you create a degree of controversy?
- How best do you keep communicating so the risks of discord are reduced?

150
Throw in the sponge too early

Beware lest you concede a point before it has been properly considered by others.

We can be disappointed by the reaction of people to our points. We think they are dismissing our observations and focusing on the reasons why we are wrong. The truth might be that they are considering the pros and cons of what we have said and reflecting on the implications. The risk is that we interpret a scowl as rejection rather than indicating careful thought. Often it will take some time before we know whether points we make are being quietly rebuffed or are shaping forward thinking.

Harry wanted to keep the goodwill of some of his colleagues because he wanted their support in areas of importance for him. He sensed that some of his proposals were not going to be readily accepted by them and had to decide how much he pressed his points and at what stage he withdrew his proposals or doubled his resolve in advocating his preferred approach. If he never changed his mind he would be regarded as belligerent but if he kept withdrawing his points he might be regarded as weak.

Reflections
- How best do you judge when to keep pressing a point and when to withdraw?
- How best do you balance being consistently pushy in certain areas and gracefully withdrawing in others?
- What emotionally might prompt you to concede a point too early?

151
Put the cart before the horse

Beware lest you try to sort out an issue before you have resolved the direction in which you want to travel.

We can get too involved in the detail of a particular plan before we have thought through what is the overall direction we are seeking to travel and what are the outcomes that are most important to us. We enjoy putting together the detailed design of next steps, but can be at risk of seeing as less important defining a way forward that has the agreement of other, major interests. Without a shared agreement about the future direction of the work the next steps can be irrelevant.

Harry was skilful on political tactics but the risk was he got into the detail too soon without building a shared understanding of the overall direction of travel and how best the different components fitted together to create the overall impact that was desired. Harry needed to focus initially on having a clear perspective for the future, with as much clarity as possible about longer-term outcomes

Reflections
* When might you go into the detailed design too quickly?
* How best do you ensure you start with the overall objective?
* Who helps you keep a focus on what you are seeking to ensure happens overall, rather than getting stuck in the detail too quickly?

152
Are burning the candle at both ends

Be mindful if you are seeking to achieve too many things within the time and energy you have got.

We want to have an impact in the organisation in which we work. We want to ensure progress in our activities both at work, in the local community and at home. We keep pushing the boundaries of what is possible and are energized by our different activities but recognise there is a limitation to our time and energy. We need to be mindful of what is giving us energy and vitality so that exhaustion does not overwhelm us.

Harry was utterly committed to his work, his community and his family and acted as if nothing was too much trouble for him. In the midst of a public holiday his energy level collapsed and he was struggling to walk around the house and garden. This was an alert that he needed to be cognisant of. This collapse in his energy had a shock effect with Harry resolving that he needed to prioritise his time and energy more deliberately. His resolve lasted for a couple of weeks.

Reflections
- When are you at risk of taking on too much responsibility?
- How best do you balance what is energizing you with the risk of exhaustion?
- When you are exhausted, how do you handle your reactions?

153
Jump the gun

Beware lest you intervene too quickly.

We have all observed individuals anxiously wanting to intervene early in a conversation. There can be a compulsiveness to express a view rather than engage with other people. They may have a good point but when it is expressed prematurely and too forcefully or anxiously, it loses its impact. Influence in a meeting is as often about the right timing and tone of an intervention.

Harry recognised his own impetuosity. He wanted to make points that were important to him and then move onto the next subject. His impatience had been both a strength and a significant weakness which led to him alienating influential people. Harry recognised that he had to hold back in meetings and judge when was the right moment to make an intervention. He used techniques like assuming that in any conversation he would be the fourth speaker, or that he would limit himself to three points, and that he would not try to solve everybody's problem for them.

Reflections
* When are you at risk of coming into a discussion too early?
* How do your emotional reactions about participating in a meeting with senior people potentially lead to misjudgements in how you intervene?
* What are the risks of intervening too late and how might that diminish your impact?

154
Are always throwing cold water

Beware the risk of always making negative points.

Cold water helps plants grow and keeps us cool in hot weather. Cold water refreshes us and enables us to be alert to what is going on around us. Throwing cold water over someone's ideas can produce an instant, negative reaction that is counter to what we might have hoped. Appropriate words of caution are worth expressing but within the context of what do we need to achieve, what is the progress we are beginning to make, and how do we best create the right sort of forward momentum.

Harry could always see the problems in implementing proposals and his experience meant he recognised pitfalls. Harry had learnt over time that he needed to interlink positive points and challenging points if they were to be constructively received. There needed to be a warmth of affirmation about progress made, before there could be serious dialogue about things he did not think were being developed as effectively as they could have been. He needed to balance reaffirming comments with one development comment if he was going to keep maintaining a positive, warm relationship.

Reflections
- How best do you balance positive and challenging comments?
- How do you advise someone who is seen as perpetually negative?
- How best do you ensure that developmental points are received in a receptive way?

155
Are seen as blind to behaviours

Beware lest a focus on outcomes means that inappropriate behaviour is legitimised.

In the heat of the moment we might make allowances for people's behaviour assuming that it follows from stress. When people are balancing difficult work and family responsibilities, we allow them the freedom to use approaches that work best for them. We can sometimes allow behaviours to slip in order to get the work done when demands are considerable. We assume that the greater good is getting an outcome delivered rather than reinforcing behaviours that are in the best interests of the organisation over the longer-term.

Harry wanted his proteges to become successful. He had encouraged them to be more assertive but received feedback that they had become aggressive rather than just assertive. Harry was reluctant to take action because he wanted to keep these young people motivated and delivering on the key issues, but he recognised that they needed to temper their approach if they were to maintain high levels of goodwill and deliver joint projects successfully.

Reflections
- When might you accept behaviours that are below what you would normally expect?
- How best do you pick up on someone's behaviour when they are under a lot of pressure to deliver?
- To what extent are you blind to the effects of your own behaviours?

156
Are seen as a flash in a pan

Beware lest you create a minor disruption which detrimentally affects forward progress.

Sometimes you might want to provoke a reaction by asking a provocative question. You want to create an immediate buzz but one provocative intervention does not necessarily enhance your long-term impact. Key is building a consistency of contribution so that you are listened to because you bring valid evidence or perspectives and not just because of a predilection to express provocative points. You want to be seen as constructive over the longer-term rather than remembered for one outlandish suggestion.

Harry recognised that when he joined any new group that he wanted to be seen to be helpful. His mind worked quickly and sometimes he was deliberately outlandish in his comments aiming to prompt some sort of forward movement. But he recognised that his long-term influence depended on engaging constructively with the ideas expressed by others and not just focused on one particular preoccupation. He also needed to adapt his style of contribution so that others were open to develop ideas with him jointly.

Reflections
- When might your interventions be received as a 'flash in the pan'?
- How best do you build consistency in your contributions?
- When is it appropriate to be provocative in waking people up to the need for action?

Bite the hand that feeds

Beware lest you take advantage of those who support you and back you.

You may have backers who promote your interest and who draw attention to your successes or help in the provision of funds for your enterprises. There might sometimes be a risk of your taking for granted their goodwill or putting expectations on them that they will find difficult to meet. When someone has been generous your demonstrating appreciation of their generosity and not assuming that it will continue for ever is going to be important. We cannot afford to lose the support and goodwill of those who speak well of us.

Harry had the support of key leaders in the Party but there was a risk that he took their support for granted and was more demanding of them in terms of their patronage and backing than they wanted to provide. When one of his sponsors told Harry that he was losing patience with him Harry recognised that he needed to check in more often with his sponsors about their perspective and concerns.

Reflections
- Which supporters might you be at risk of taking advantage of or annoying?
- When is it unreasonable to expect someone's goodwill towards you to continue indefinitely?
- How do you recover from a rebuff when a sponsor signals that you had been expecting too much of them?

158
Count your chickens before they hatch

Beware lest you assume your preferred action will happen before full agreement has been reached.

We think that significant progress has been made with key people in alignment. We judge that there is very little that can now get in the way of a successful outcome. But until a final declaration has been, or the contract had been signed, there is no guarantee about the outcome. It is helpful in motivating others to describe significant progress but success only comes when the finishing line is crossed.

Harry sometimes used the technique of describing an agreement as having been reached when it was only 90% there. He did this deliberately to build an assumption that there was no point in people continuing to oppose a particular outcome. Harry recognised that sometimes he could overdo this technique. He was honest enough with himself to know that on some occasions it was going to be counterproductive to assume an agreed outcome before everyone had endorsed his favoured approach.

Reflections
- When are you at risk of assuming agreement has been reached when there are continuing uncertainties?
- How useful is it sometimes to be assuming full agreement before all have endorsed an approach?
- How best do you distinguish between a trend you can affirm and a way forward that needs to be formally agreed with others?

159
Judge a book by its cover

Beware lest you make judgements based on appearances rather than careful analysis.

We want an initiative to be successful and are at risk of just seeing the positive in each step. Or we are sceptical about a particular initiative and see the negative in each contribution. We may make judgements based on how an initiative is presented rather than focusing on the longer-term impact of what is proposed. We may be very quick to make judgements and say that we will consider the detail later.

Harry enjoyed meeting new people but tended to make instant judgements about people based on his first interaction. This gave him a useful starting point in assessing how seriously he needed to take observations from individuals. He recognised he could write people off too quickly if they did not interact with him as well as he would have hoped. He also recognised that he could believe people too readily without checking out how reliable their judgements were.

Reflections
- When are you at risk of judging people too quickly?
- How best do you ensure that your view of someone is not based just on an initial interaction?
- How best do you recover when you made an initial judgement about somebody which proves wrong?

160
Disappear without trace

Beware lest you disappear at moments when you can be influential.

During my time as the Finance Director General for a UK Government Department my key interlocutor at the Treasury had a tendency to disappear at moments when I most needed to talk with her. I was frustrated when she was not available at key moments, but she was deliberate in not being available when she was not in a position to say anything definitive. I felt frustrated by her capacity to disappear without trace at regular intervals, but she probably felt as equally frustrated with me for being persistent in wanting to seek an up-to-date perspective about thinking within the Treasury.

Harry used to disappear without trace sometimes in order to preserve his energy. He did not want to be constantly available to people who were wanting to persuade him to do things that were not within his control to deliver. He recognised that he could not disappear all the time and needed to be explicit when he was available to talk to people and then be committed to being available at those times.

Reflections
* When is it helpful to disappear for a period?
* When can disappearing regularly undermine your credibility and influence with others?
* How best do you communicate clearly why you are disappearing for a period?

161
Be captive to your former self

Beware lest an earlier version of you dictates your current and future actions.

Deeply embedded in us are approaches and mindsets that come from past experiences. In earlier phases we might have been excessively deferential or too self-opinionated. When the pressure is on, we might revert to a previous version of ourselves and display behaviours and approaches that we thought we had left behind. We had not been liberated from these earlier versions of ourselves in the way that we had hoped. Perhaps we need trusted colleagues to tell us that an earlier version of ourselves is beginning to creep out.

In his twenties Harry was a dogmatic, fiery politician who railed against injustice. A consequence of taking on different leadership responsibilities was that he became much collaborative and recognised that he needed to respect and draw in people with different views to his own. He saw this directness as a valuable part of his armoury but recognised that he needed to keep it firmly under control. He did not want to lose the support of those he had spent hours building an understanding with.

Reflections
- When might emotional reactions from the past resurface?
- How aware are you about when you might be demonstrating a former version of yourself?
- When is it useful to bring out qualities that were dominant in a former version of yourself?

162
Jump in where angels fear to tread

Be watchful when you enter an opinion when those with most experience are holding back.

We decide that we need to point out the obvious way forward and are surprised when we are ignored. We wonder why some of the experienced people around us are not contributing. Perhaps there is something we do not know or history that is evident to others and not to us. When we have made our point, we stand back, observe and wait to see if anything happens. Perhaps it will in due time, but we are conscious that there may be sensitivities that we are blind to.

Harry did not have an abundance of patience. When people seem to be delicately walking around a subject, he wanted to make the obvious points recognising that there could be an adverse reaction. Sometimes this approach meant his views were dismissed or ignored. On other occasions, his comments forced into the open an issue that needed addressing more effectively. Harry did not always get this judgement right but recognised that part of his leadership contribution was to state obvious, unsaid facts.

Reflections
- When might you speak the truth knowing that it will not be well received by everyone?
- How do you balance watching and observing alongside saying what needs to be said?
- When do you gracefully retreat?

163
Shoot the messenger

Beware lest you criticise or castigate the bearer of bad news.

It can be a brave act to bring bad news to people longing for a positive outcome. You recognise that the instant reaction might be a deluge of words with your feeling aggrieved by their apparent criticism of you. You try to position yourself as the messenger and not the advocate of this particular way forward. You recognise that sometimes you have to absorb the angst to enable someone to work through their pain or disgust. You are mindful that it is not helpful to protest back to the individual how you are experiencing their reaction.

Harry recognised that he could display quite a fiery reaction when told bad news. It helped if he was forewarned that he was about to receive a difficult piece of news. He would then steel himself and prepare his emotions so that he considered rationally the news he was being given. When given bad news unexpectedly he knew he had to absorb the information and not instantly react by establishing the facts clearly and saying that he would work out his response in due time.

Reflections
- When might you be at risk of 'shooting the messenger'?
- How best do you prepare to receive difficult news?
- What enables you to convey bad news for others and be prepared for a painful reaction?

164
Be a slave to ambition

Beware if ambition dictates your every action.

Every organisation needs people with ambition who can see future opportunities and move an organisation on constructively. Individual ambition expressed in the right way can have a powerful beneficial effect enabling an organisation to deliver its purpose in a dynamic and effective way, but ambition that focuses on self-interest can soon become destructive and lead to wariness and limited trust from others. If ambition shapes every decision it can be counterproductive in overriding key values and damage relationships

Harry had always been ambitious about reaching a senior role in his political Party dating from his student days. He had had a plan in his mind about the steps he wanted to take and was deliberate in the relationships he built and the responsibilities he was willing to take on. When this planned sequence was thwarted by events outside his control, he became cross with both himself and the Party. It was a rude awakening that others were not just going to allow his ambition to determine their decisions. He needed to be more patient and adaptable in taking forward his ambition.

Reflections
* When does a sense of ambition enable your organisation to think forward constructively?
* When has your ambition given you a sense of purpose?
* How do you respond when your ambition is thwarted?

Lessons from Shakespeare

165
Delays have dangerous ends

A delay is a decision not to proceed or to postpone or slow down action.

Delay is an essential tool when awaiting information being available or alignment being built in support of a forward direction. But one delay after another can lead to disenchantment and the sapping of energy and resolve. Perpetual delay means that opportunities are missed and allows others to take the initiative. Delaying for too long waiting for supportive information can mean we are blinded to reality going on around us and are consequently left dangerously exposed to criticism of wilful blindness or destructive inactivity.

Carol recognised that the finances of the charity she led were not strong and recognised the need to restructure the organisation. There were always reasons to delay decisions and Carol was reluctant to take the hard steps that were needed. When giving to the charity dropped significantly because of the Covid-19 pandemic Carol regretted that she had not made the necessary structural changes earlier. Her decision not to restructure meant that the charity was in a more precarious position than if she had acted using her best judgement at an earlier stage.

Reflection
* When has delay led to a better outcome or a poorer outcome?
* How best do you look ahead to see the consequences of delay?
* How do you differentiate between a good delay and a risky delay?

166
Blown with the windy tempest of my heart

Be alert lest your emotions dictate your actions.

You are passionate about taking forward a particular idea. You see all the objections as misconceived. On other occasions you feel strongly that a decision should not be taken and you use all the arguments you can think of to undermine the course of action favoured by others. In both situations you display an energy which can border on the tempestuous. Heart is leading head: your approach may be right or might be misguided. You are at risk of not thinking through the implications of your emotive interventions.

Carol could become very passionate about initiatives that the charity should take forward. There was a strong, emotional connectivity between her and the pain of the people the charity was seeking to serve. What mattered was doing the best that the charity could for those suffering hardship. This passion in Carol's heart attracted donors and motivated the volunteers. The passion sometimes became a whirlwind with the risk that the passion of one month dwarfed the passion of the preceding month.

Reflections
- When does your passion invigorate others?
- When are you at risk of moving too quickly from one passion to another?
- How can you direct your passion to best long-term effect?

My salad days when I was green in judgement

It can be helpful to remind yourself what approaches you took when you were younger.

In your early working life, you may have been enthused by a sense of purpose and intrigued by progress that could be made. You brought an innocence about what was possible and were not prejudging using past experience about what was feasible. You brought a fresh approach unchallenged by prejudice or previous bruising. Sometimes it can help to remind ourselves of how a younger version of ourselves might have reacted in a similar situation.

Carol readily recalled how she felt as a field officer in a charity in her twenties. Her enthusiasm showed no bounds and her ability to get alongside people meant she built constructive alliances. In later years Carol had become more wary about the motives of different people. Carol reminded herself that from time to time that she needed to apply her capacity to draw out the best in others in the way she built forward relationships, while still keeping an element of wariness in her approach.

Reflections
- What might a younger version of yourself be thinking and doing in your current situation?
- What characterised your mind-set in your twenties that is still pertinent now?
- What makes you wary about applying the same approach now which you brought in your twenties?

168
From hour to hour we ripe and ripe. And then from hour to hour we rot and rot

We can't stand still. We are either growing or diminishing, and can be doing both at the same time in different areas of our lives.

We are either going forwards or backwards. We are either increasing in understanding, wisdom and effectiveness, or we are becoming set in our ways, limited in our perspective and closed to new possibilities. We can influence whether we are keeping growing in understanding and when we begin to close our minds to opportunities. Self-awareness is key in helping us decide when we need to change our approach or to move on.

Carol was now working in her fourth charity. She was mindful that she needed to feel that she was growing in understanding and effectiveness if she was going to remain enthusiastic about the work she was doing. She had seen too many people stay in a specific charity role for too long and become rigid in their thinking, beleaguered in their approach and resenting their lack of career progression.

Reflections
- What helps you keep thinking forward bringing out the best in yourself and others?
- How do you ensure that you do not close in on yourself and cease to look forward constructively?
- How best do you enable others to ripen and not rot?

169
Brevity is the soul of wit

The shortest interventions are often the most effective contributions.

The most effective contributors to meetings are often those who make short, poignant and timely contributions. They draw attention to a key piece of information, a likely consequence, or a hidden risk. A good intervention might seek to slow a conversation down and suggest a key question. It is the quality of an intervention that matters and not its quantity. Your objective may be to encourage people to think ahead and to work through the consequences of your contribution. An instant answer is not needed if the objective is to shift people's thinking.

Carol recognised that sometimes she talked too much. She particularly valued discussion with her Board Chair who would listen carefully to what she said and then give her insightful observations or pose questions that helped Carol shape her thinking going forward. Carol knew that the Chair's comments would be pertinent and would help her begin to develop her next steps. Carol tried hard to keep her interventions focused, but knew that she would never be fully successful in this intent.

Reflections
- Who do you observe making brief, timely and influential interjections?
- When can brevity be your greatest asset?
- When is it helpful to be identifying the key question rather than set out a lengthy solution?

170
By indirections find directions out

When one route proves to be wrong it gives us information which helps us find a better route.

Sometimes action is better than indecision to test out whether a particular route is going to be productive or not. When a particular approach is not working well, we ask ourselves what is our learning and how best can I use that understanding to inform the approach that I now decide to embark on. The most powerful insights often flow from the learning from choices that have not worked out as well as we had hoped.

Carol came to recognise that her time at one charity, which had been painful at the time, had developed in her a resilience and an ability to take difficult decisions which had been hugely beneficial in subsequent roles. What had felt a painful experience was a key formative influence on her leadership. At the time the experience had seemed wasteful and debilitating. In retrospect the experience had had long-term, profound benefits for her in developing her leadership acumen.

Reflections
- How best do you recover and embrace learning from decisions that proved wrong?
- How best do you leave any debilitating sense of failure behind?
- What enables you to be philosophic about decisions you took that did not lead to the outcomes you had hoped for?

171
The wheel has come full circle

Sometimes you come back to the point where you began.

You set off with energy and expectancy but events do not unfold in the way you hoped. You seek to be philosophic that you need to start again. You dig deep into your reserves and recognise that you need to begin again with renewed energy informed by what had gone wrong and seeking to bring a fresh approach. You accept that you might have to keep coming back to the same starting point until you find a way forward that is effective and sustainable.

Carol recognised that a couple of her trustees were keen on a particular venture. Carol had reservations but concluded that she needed to seek to take forward what the trustees wanted to see developed. Eventually these two trustees accepted that their preferred approach was not going to work and recognised that the discussion about finding the best approach needed to start again. The upside was that these trustees were now more openminded about next steps.

Reflections
- When do you need to graciously accept that you are back at the starting point?
- How do you enable people to appreciate their learning when they need to start again on a particular initiative?
- When do you allow yourself to recognise that coming back to the starting point is the best option?

172
There is no virtue like necessity

Necessity is a valuable starting point.

We can be full of aspirations and hopes. We want to take forward opportunities and build a better organisation or deliver more effective outcomes. What may need to come first is addressing necessity. Until the finances are sorted out or certain personnel issues are resolved, progress is unlikely. Blockages have to be tackled and removed, and distrust resolved before there can be any reasonable prospect of forward movement. An external crisis can create the opportunity for radical rethinking and restructuring that had previously seemed unattainable.

Carol recognised that the age profile of the donors meant that giving from existing donors was likely to diminish and not grow. Carol saw as a basic necessity that the charity looked again at its donor structure and put greater emphasis on both attracting younger donors and focusing on inviting retired supporters to consider including the charity in their wills. A cliff edge was about to appear in donor income unless quick action was taken.

Reflections
- Do you see necessity as an essential starting point or a distraction?
- How do you link necessity to the forward direction of an organisation?
- When might necessity overwhelm you and limit your aspirations unnecessarily?

173
More in sorrow than anger

A strong emotion might best be expressed as sorrow rather than anger.

When something goes wrong different emotions can kick in. It might sometimes be an emotion of crossness, frustration and anger. On other occasions, the dominant emotion might be one of sadness or sorrow. When something goes wrong there will inevitably be an emotional reaction, perhaps over time we can steer ourselves towards a reaction of sadness and sorrow rather than anger and frustration. The emotion of sadness and sorrow enables us to come to accept what has happened and begin to think into how we handle the situation going forward. It helps us move through disappointment into a more constructive frame of mind towards the future.

Carol knew that she could feel aggrieved when mistakes are made. She had trained herself to be calm when something went wrong and to express her concerns as a thoughtful reflection rather than overt disappointment. She had learnt over time that being gracious in her reactions and thoughtful in working through next steps was much more likely to create the right sort of learning than a deluge of angry words.

Reflections
- How best do you slow down your reaction to bad news?
- How might you turn a desire to be angry into an expression of sadness or sorrow?
- How best do you handle disappointment?

174
Hoist with his own petard

Be mindful when your strongly held views might be turned against you.

You insist that clear evidence is needed before a particular action advocated by a colleague should be agreed. A few weeks later the colleague uses the same argument with you that you had used with him a few weeks earlier. You accept that there is no point in complaining about your colleague's approach and decide that you have to respond constructively to him and collect more data before you can reasonably expect a decision to be taken.

Carol was adamant that a particular decision was justified on the basis of fairly limited evidence. Her trustees were more sceptical. Underlying this hesitation was the feeling amongst some trustees that their ideas were too quickly dismissed by Carol without being thoroughly tested. Carol accepted that it was inconsistent for her to be dismissive of suggestions from trustees and then insist that her favoured way forward was right on the basis of her intuitive understanding rather than testing out ideas in a pilot study.

Reflections
- How might you respond when people deploy with you the same rationale that you use with them?
- When you make a strongly worded statement based on your values, how do you assess how others experience the way you live those values?
- When might you be inconsistent in your expectations on others and yourself?

Our attitude of mind

175
Let a thousand flowers bloom

Encourage a range of different possibilities and see which ones catch the imagination.

There are times when it is not clear what is the right idea to take forward. You want to encourage thinking about a range of different possibilities to see which ones prove attractive and worthwhile. You watch how different suggestions garner support and interest, and which ones seem to be developing constructively. You take delight if there is enthusiasm for some ideas and recognise that other possibilities might be gaining less interest or traction.

Brenda was conscious that her teams wanted to operate differently in a post Covid-19 world. Some would want to ensure that their team meetings were face to face while other teams had got used to virtual team meetings and had built a rhythm that worked well for them. Other teams might want to use a mixture of face to face and virtual. Brenda did not want to set out a fixed, formulaic approach to how the teams organised themselves. She worked with the team leaders to devise prompts about good practice to ensure all team members were fully engaged.

Reflections
- What flexibilities do you want to advocate in ways of working?
- How comfortable are you if people come up with very different ways of tackling issues?
- How ready are you to accept different teams having very different approaches?

176
The road not taken

When you make choices, we need to accept that we are foregoing other possibilities.

There is a risk that we can dwell too much on roads we decided not to take. We wonder what the outcomes might have been if we had made different choices. We remind ourselves that agonising over what might have been drains our energy and can create a negative spiral. We accept that we need to appreciate our contentedness in where we are now and see possibilities and opportunities going forward recognising what we have learnt through the various decisions we have taken in life.

Brenda had started in an acting career with moderate success. After a series of disappointments, she joined the Civil Service where her ability to communicate clearly and persuasively enabled her to move quickly into positions of responsibility. When she hankered to be back on the theatre stage, she reminded herself that she was now operating on a wider platform where skills she had learnt in her acting training and experience were immensely useful as she sought to be a persuasive presence in many different meetings.

Reflections
- When am I at risk of regretting past decisions?
- How best do I ensure that I recognise the pluses that have flowed from career choices?
- What helps me limit any sense of disappointment about past decisions?

177
See life as a marathon and not a sprint

The importance of bringing a longer-term perspective rather than just dwelling on the immediate

We can become preoccupied in the here and now. We want to put energy into making changes happen now and having the satisfaction of immediate results. But we recognise that we can exhaust ourselves and set our expectations too narrowly. We are reminded that we need to be seeing life in decades and not days, and be deliberate about developing our understanding and our garnering of insights and energy for the longer term.

Brenda was determined to make a success of her current role. Because she was always willing to take on responsibilities, expectations were placed upon her. Brenda recognised that she had to be more deliberate in thinking about next steps in her career and the skills and experiences she needed to enhance. She accepted that it was better to be developing her repertoire of leadership approaches in different contexts rather than pushing for early promotion. She did not want to either exhaust herself or be stereotyped as a fixer in solving short-term issues.

Reflections
- When might you be too preoccupied with the short-term?
- What will help you pace yourself for the longer term?
- How do you want to develop a repertoire of leadership approaches needed for the longer-term?

178
Take the lid off

After a piece of good news encourage people to be excited about future possibilities.

We recognise that initial indications of progress are reassuring but are not guarantees of success. We know we have to be patient in waiting for evidence before we know that there has been a significant shift in people's thinking or behaviour. But marking initial signs of progress can release people to see significant progress as possible.

Brenda had initiated a number of pilot studies testing out different ways of analysing data and responding to customers. She was delighted when there were initial indications from one team that they were relishing the opportunity to do things differently and use data in a different way. This team was not now inhibited. It saw possibilities ahead and was enthusing other teams about possible future opportunities. Brenda allowed herself an inner smile about this progress while recognising that celebrating a transformed approach was some time way.

Reflections
- Allow yourself to enjoy initial signs of progress
- See first indications of progress as opening up the prospect of significant changes
- Encourage people to be enthused about what can be achieved

179
Look through the other end of the telescope

It can be helpful to look from the future into the past to see the journey travelled.

It can be helpful to imagine ourselves in the future looking back on where we have come from and the different stages in our journey. When we look back we observe how our beliefs, attitudes and approaches have evolved. We have moved forward, be it in uneven steps, with learning from what has gone well and less well. We are encouraged by our journey and philosophic about when we made the wrong turning or got stuck.

Brenda recognised that she could become disappointed in herself. Sometimes she needed to look back and see how her different experiences had developed her as a leader and as an effective team member. She smiled at her innocent mistakes in the past and recognised that life had taught her many lessons about protecting herself from the unreasonable expectations of others and how best to develop the influence and impact that she most wanted to achieve.

Reflections
* Can you see your journey so far in a positive way with learning at each step?
* How best do you interpret previous disappointments?
* When you look back from the future to where you are now, how does that influence the way you spend your time and energy?

180
Watch getting caught in the vortex

The excitement of being at the centre of action can be exhausting and debilitating.

We enjoy being busy and being part of the action. We know there is a risk that we get so absorbed in the intensity of the moment that our reserves of energy are rapidly diminished and we can move from a sense of ecstatic engagement to devastating exhaustion. When caught in the intensity of the vortex we can be blinded to the effect on our wellbeing and unable to see clearly the consequences on ourselves.

Government Ministers expected Brenda to both solve short-term problems and to be developing longer-term approaches. The risk was she was drawn into the short-term because of the immediate expectations of Ministers, with long-term considerations having less attention. Brenda knew that when the immediate crisis was over that the Ministers would not accept that their immediate expectations had meant that Brenda had only had time for finding short-term solutions. Brenda knew she had to manage her time and energy to continuing to address longer-term issues and not be completely dominated by the vortex of the immediate.

Reflections
- When might you be too caught up in the immediate?
- How best do you ration your time and energy between the immediate the longer-term?
- What are the danger signs that you are enjoying the vortex of the immediate too much?

Watch dwelling on broken dreams

View past disappointments as providing insights and not a cause of regret.

Dreams about the future give us hope and a sense of purpose and help shape our aspirations and sense of direction. Dreams about the contribution we can make to assist others can inspire us. Many dreams don't happen for a myriad of reasons. Sometimes a dream seems plausible but then is shattered by circumstances beyond our control. We recognise the risk of being too preoccupied with a past aspiration that has not materialised.

Brenda had dreamt about running her own organisation and relished the prospect of a significant degree of independence. In mid-career she had to come to terms with a health issue which meant that she could become exhausted very quickly. She decided that one way forward was to become part of a job-share. She turned the prospect of working three days a week from a sign of weakness into a positive recognition of her health situation. With an effective job-share partner she now saw the prospect of being able to become a CEO of a significant organisation. A dream that felt broken in her mind might yet be possible..

Reflections
- What broken dreams might you overly dwell on?
- When has a broken dream helped reshape our aspirations for the future?
- What enables you to be philosophic about broken dreams from the past?

182
Beware being caught in a huddle of anger

Anger can be contagious, inflammatory and destructive.

When we feel a sense of anger, we want to express it in a way that releases emotion. We have learnt that this is best done alone or with a trusted friend. We are conscious that anger in a group can soon escalate and create an intensity of resentment with frustrations bursting out in unhelpful and potentially destructive ways. Anger soon magnifies into resentment and aggressive words that are easily said and have long-term destructive consequences.

Brenda observed that there was a growing resentment amongst a group in the wider organisation who felt misunderstood and misinterpreted. This group felt they had been blamed for decisions that had gone wrong and that senior management were distancing themselves from this group. Brenda was deliberate in seeking to help them come to terms with understanding what had happened and move into a less tempestuous place. She sought to bring a calmness while listening hard to their concerns.

Reflections
- When might anger begin to overwhelm a group?
- How best do you draw the sting out of the anger in groups you work with?
- When might your own anger inhibit you from enabling others to deal effectively with the anger they are addressing?

183
The blame-game is easy and self-destructive

Blaming others can mean you avoid taking responsibility for your actions.

Blaming others can be an easy way of creating an explanation about events that went wrong. It enables you to have no sense of responsibility for your own actions and, therefore no regrets about the past and no inhibitions about the future. Blaming others can lead to writing them off or demonising them, which inhibits the possibility of constructive working together going forward. Leaping to blame limits the opportunity to look as objectively as possible at what happened and what the learning is for the future.

Brenda felt badly let down by some colleagues who had promised to deliver and failed to do so. Part of her recognised that she carried some responsibility. She had not been as close to these colleagues as she might have been and had not interpreted some of the early warnings as clearly as she might have done about risks and misalignment. Brenda recognised her desire to blame her colleagues, alongside the need to accept that she could have done things differently which might have limited some of the change.

Reflections
- When might blaming others be an easy and self-destructive approach?
- When you want to blame others, how do you catch that emotional reaction early?
- How best do you respond to others when they appear to want to blame you and your people?

184
The puzzled shrug of the shoulders

Beware the impression that you don't understand and you don't care.

Our body language is being observed and interpreted all the time. The shrug of the shoulders could indicate disinterest, boredom or uncertainty. The impression might be entirely different to our intent, hence the importance of recognising the signals that our body language gives and thinking through how best we monitor our own body language and are deliberate in the impressions we give so that we do not inadvertently give signals that we might later regret.

Brenda knew that when she was uncertain her shoulders sagged and she could look unconfident. She had learnt that she needed to articulate clearly how she was responding so that others did not misinterpret the way she held herself and looked at them. There were times she needed to relax her shoulders and be very engaging in conversation. There were moments to hold her shoulders back and be focused and deliberate in what she said and how she demonstrated a forward sense of purpose.

Reflections
- How do people interpret your natural pose in meetings?
- When are you at risk of giving unhelpful or false signals through the way you sit and engage?
- What will help you use your shoulders in signalling the tone you want to set?

SECTION H

Eternal truths

185
As you make your bed you must lie on it

Once we have made choices we have to live with the consequences.

We like to explore different options and taste different possibilities. Our curiosity takes us in different directions and we do not want to be constrained in how we spend our time and energy. We want to retain our adaptability in the way we think and we recognise that we have to live with the consequences of our decisions if we want to maintain our income, our relationships and our home, even though in retrospect they may seem suboptimal in some respects

Rashid liked the variety that came with working as a management consultant. He could dabble in other people's issues, express a view and not have responsibility for implementing ideas. He recognised that he had to live with the inevitable uncertainties that flowed from being a consultant as the work could dry up at any moment. He had learnt to live with the unpredictability of his income and the lack of long-term engagement with particular topics. This was a reasonable trade-off for doing work he really enjoyed.

Reflections
- How best do you live with choices you made in the past that were suboptimal?
- How readily do you recognise choices that have long-term consequences?
- How best do you see good in situations which are sub-optimal?

186
Cut your coat according to your cloth

A dose of realism is needed in recognising the limitations of what is available to us.

We want to be ambitious and change the organisation we are part of for good. We want to take forward radical ideas that we believe will make a significant different. We see an opportunity that should be attractive to colleagues. We are disappointed when our ideas don't gain support. We need to combine being bold and pragmatic. When we see an opportunity, we need to be deliberate in assessing how many allies we have. When we see the need for investment, we need to be honest in assessing the resources available to us.

Rashid could see clearly how the consultancy could have a big impact in the Insurance business as he had seen the contrast between good practice and poor management. He had lots of constructive ideas but the reception to his plea for significant investment was lukewarm. Reluctantly he accepted that he needed to move a step at a time and demonstrate as a result of initial recruitment that the business was growing in the Insurance market. Only then would there be the prospect of a significant scaling up in the Insurance area.

Reflections
- How best do you combine being bold and pragmatic?
- How best do you temper your own enthusiasms into practical steps?
- What enables you to make the most of limited resources?

187
Withdraw gracefully

There are times when the best action is measured withdrawal.

You believe that a particular course of action is needed and set out the reasons for your preferred decisions. Others are more sceptical and raise points that don't convince you. Perhaps your colleagues need time to weigh up the evidence and become comfortable with different options going forward. You decide to hold back from pushing your points and conclude that it would be better to wait until certain events have unfolded. You recognise that now is not the moment to push for a decision because it may produce the wrong answer.

Rashid saw scope to expand in the Health sector. His colleagues were sceptical because the profit margin was bigger in the commercial sector than in the public sector. Rashid recognised that if he pressed the point about a major expansion in the Health sector, he would not get the full backing at this time. He needed to develop the case further with clearer examples of where focused consultancy support could make a significant difference with a convincing narrative about value for money.

Reflections
- When are you likely to see withdrawal as defeat?
- How best do you withdraw gracefully?
- How readily do you recognise when it is better to hold back than press for a decision that might go against your favoured approach?

188
Don't carry all your eggs in one basket

Allow yourself to believe that there can be more than one potential way forward.

When exploring two or three different options it is helpful to weigh up comparative merits and downsides. When addressing a difficult issue, it is useful to explore more than one way of solving an issue to avoid becoming too wedded to a particular set of steps. When building allies for a particular course of action, it is worth investing in conversation with a number of different people rather than relying just on previous supporters.

Rashid could see how investment in one sector was likely to lead to a higher rate of return than investment in other sectors. However, experience had taught him that the market changed rapidly and the consultancy business needed to have credibility in a number of sectors as there was inevitably going to be significant fluctuations in demand. Rashid recognised that choices would need to be made but he needed to be selective, and not close down too many possibilities.

Reflections
* When are you at risk of being too focused on one way forward?
* How best do you limit but not over constrain your options going forward?
* How best do you hold onto to potential future options?

189
Every cloud has a silver lining

Always look for potentially positive developments in any acute problem or crisis.

When I am working alongside someone going through a difficult time, I try to choose a good moment to ask what might be the changes in their mindsets they might make or the opening up of different choices that can be taken forward. Perhaps there has been an increased flexibility in the way people have responded. Asking what is one good thing that has come out of a difficult situation can bring a new perspective to a painful and apparently debilitating set of circumstances.

Rashid was often having conversations with his colleagues about projects that had not gone as well as they had hoped. Rashid became adept at helping to turn round someone's perspective so that they could articulate what they had learnt through handling a particular project and how they would approach next steps in a different way taking account of insights that had only gradually become apparent. Rashid was a natural optimist, but knew he had to temper that optimism while fully understanding the concerns that his colleagues had about what had gone wrong.

Reflections
- How do you allow yourself to believe that every cloud has a silver lining?
- How best do you draw the positive out of negative experiences?
- How best do you temper optimism with an honest assessment of what has gone wrong?

190
Experience teaches fools

However foolish we might feel, experience is always teaching us wisdom.

Hindsight allows us to see the folly of our ways. We look back on foolish things we did and said that gave us or others unnecessary angst or pain, while recognising that through our foolish acts our sensitivities and insights have been shaped. Foolishness is the precursor to wisdom. We hope that our foolishness has not led to too many casualties and that we have not harmed ourselves in a way that has caused long-term damage.

Rashid occasionally reminded himself of the sequence of foolish decisions he had taken. At the time he was doing what he thought was right but in retrospect he had misjudged interventions and decisions. But against most foolish acts he was able to identify one good thing that had flowed from his foolishness. In some cases, his vulnerability had endeared him to others and built a strong connectivity with them. On other occasions his foolishness had taught him not to do something in the same way on future occasions. Rashid accepted that he should regard hs foolish traits as endearing and unfortunate rather than terminal.

Reflections
- What have you learnt about yourself from foolish acts?
- How much has your foolishness shaped your perspective going forward?
- How understanding are you of other people's foolishness?

191
Pride comes before a fall

When we are most pleased with ourselves we might be less observant about the potential pitfalls around us.

It is right to take pride in the contribution we are able to make and to be able to sum up our approach in a constructive way. The risk comes when we believe that our way is the only way and that our success cannot be replicated by others. Self-confidence enables us to be bold. If we are over self-confident we can become blinkered. There can be moments when we are blinded by our own self-belief and not aware we are losing support from others.

Rashid recognised that he had to balance confidence in advocating a narrative for the future of the business while at the same time listening hard to what others were saying. He needed to be bold enough to advocate a way forward and humble enough to recognise that he might have got it wrong and that others could improve on his ideas. He needed to take pride in the way he listened and adapted to changing circumstances.

Reflections
- When might your boldness have blinkered you to risks?
- How best do you take pride in what you are doing and continue to be open-minded?
- Who tells you if your pride in what you are doing borders on blindness to what other people are saying?

192
Turkeys don't vote for Christmas

Be alert to when self-interest colours peoples' judgements.

You expect your colleagues to be looking at options and future possibilities in the most objective way possible weighing up the evidence and being dispassionate about the pros and cons of different choices. If staff numbers are to be reduced you hope your team leaders will be thinking about what is in the best interest of the enterprise. You recognise that you need to discount in some ways their perspectives because an element of self-interest in inevitably going to have an influence in the way they assess options.

Rashid wanted to remove a layer of middle management in one sphere of activity. Many of the responses from team leaders were predictable and were strongly influenced by self-interest. A couple of colleagues were more dispassionate in the way they assessed the implications. Rashid recognised he needed to accept that people's personal positions would colour their reactions and that he needed to try and identify those who had views that were more balanced to help him think through next steps.

Reflections
* When might our views be distorted by self-interest?
* How best do we take account of self-interest distorting the perspective of others?
* When do we need to be overt about parking self-interest?

193
Remove the beam from your eye first

We need to remove the blockages in our thinking before we criticize the limitations in the perspective of others.

You are ready to criticise someone else's approach on a relatively minor point but there might be an even bigger flaw in the way you are looking at reality. We need others to tell us what might be distorting our vision and where our niggling away at fallacies in other people's thinking might be undermining our credibility.

Rashid kept suggesting that the consultants in different geographic areas were not talking to each other at an early enough stage and were not keeping up to speed with what was happening in other economics. What the area leads wanted was a much clearer sense of forward direction from Rashid and clarity about how the performance of individual areas would be judged. Rashid was reluctant to accept that part of the problem was his lack of articulation of clear, overriding priorities.

Reflections
- When might you focus too much on what others are doing because it is not quite how you would have done it?
- What can get in the way of your having a clear, forward perspective?
- Who do you legitimise telling you when your vision is distorted?

194
Fire is a good servant and a bad master

Beware lest an approach that works well in one context becomes over dominant in determining your way forward.

A particular form of analysis provides you with valuable data and you come to rely heavily upon it. You want to use analysis in different areas but recognise that you could become a slave to a particular approach and become over dependent on the proponents of that approach. Key is keeping alert to when we might become over dominated by one influential group or approach.

Rashid would deliberately bring people together to focus on an issue. He wanted to create good dialogue which enabled options to be explored rigorously, but he also knew that he did not want that dialogue to get out of hand. He wanted people to be open, frank, exploratory and challenging of each other, but he did not want debate to turn into fiery exchanges. He was deliberate in moderating conversations so they were honest and supportive with people's views being respected as well as challenged.

Reflections
- When do you need to get people engaged in frank, open dialogue?
- How best do you ensure honest, frank challenge that does not become personal or destructive?
- How do you turn up the heat while ensuring people are not burnt?

195
He who pays the piper calls the tune

Those funding an enterprise largely determine its future direction.

A charity chief executive may have grand ideas about where they want to take the charity, but they are subject to what the donors are prepared to fund. There may be advocates within an organisation to invest in a particular area, but key will be decisions by the Executive Team about priorities for the use of both people and financial resources. There can be strong advocacy for the pursuit of particular possibilities alongside an unrealism about funding.

Rashid wanted to give people the freedom to think in fresh ways. He knew that tough decisions would always be needed about where to invest. He wanted people to use their freedom to develop ideas but he needed a tight, disciplined approach when it came to the allocation of resources. He did not want to make every decision on resourcing, but there needed to be a clear process with a limited number of people involved so that resources were allocated in a deliberate and objective way.

Reflections
- How realistic are you in assessing who makes decisions on resourcing?
- When should you be more deliberate in making decisions on finance and not allow others to make them for you?
- When might you be at risk of wanting to be over prescriptive in decisions on resources?

196
It's a long lane with no turning

Opportunities can appear when you had not expected them.

We see a clear direction in front of us which can feel remorseless and boring. But the unexpected happens and there is a choice to be made. Life is not quite as remorselessly dull as we had expected. Perhaps we have had opportunities we had not expected, or events in our lives have not turned out as we would have hoped and there are difficult circumstances to face into. We had not foreseen that we would need to change and adapt the way we spend our time.

Rashid could see his way ahead in developing his consultancy business. It was going to be worthwhile if a bit dull over the next few months, but he had learnt from experience that events would always happen that would disrupt the way forward. The unexpected downturn of business in a particular area was initially a shock, but it gave an impetus to redeploy staff. This was a reminder to Rashid of how unpredictable the pathway ahead looked: he needed to keep a constant eye out for opportunities and risks.

Reflections
- When might you be overconfident about the course you are set on?
- What will help you look out for new opportunities when you are set on a particular way forward?
- When do you view possible turnings as distractions or encouragements?

Sauce for the goose is sauce for the gander

Remember that concessions for one group will be seen as the rights for another group.

You may be reliant on the economists in shaping forward investment: hence you back this group with resources and affirmation. Other groups become a shade envious of the apparent favouritism being given to the economists. You are conscious that you need to give affirmation in appropriate ways to different groups recognising what they are contributing. You recognise that you have to be hard-nosed about the use of resources so that they are allocated in a way that meets the best long-term interest of the business.

Rashid was conscious that his people kept a careful watch on how different parts of the organisation were being funded. Rashid recognised that he could not let special pleading for resources from one area legitimise everyone else feeling they had a right to a similar level or resources. He knew he had to be selective in the way he allocated resources and communicate clearly why he was making the decisions that he did.

Reflections
- How clearly do you communicate your reasons when you are putting more investment into one area rather than another?
- How do you affirm different contributions while being differential in the way you allocate resources?
- How sensitive are you to undercurrents about unfairness and equal treatment?

198
Life is not a dress rehearsal

Every decision we make has consequences.

There are times when we need to sit lightly to what we are doing, recognising that our choices and our influence are in real time. Our engagement in work and life is not a theoretical endeavour. We are influencing people and situations for good or ill. Every word we say or action we take has consequences. We are not rehearsing for a play that may or may not happen in the future: we are part of the action now with an influence. We are on a stage being observed. There is a stark reality in everything we do that we cannot avoid.

Rashid knew that every decision he took would have consequences for individuals when he decided to invest in one area and reduce investment in another. He needed to explain his decisions because they had a real impact on people's lives. This was not a dress rehearsal or a theoretical exercise. He needed to ensure that the business generated income if there were to be interesting and worthwhile jobs for people going forward.

Reflections
- How can you combine taking decisions seriously with sitting lightly to the responsibilities you carry?
- How best do you see each stage you are engaged in as an act in an unfolding play?
- When might you rehearse in order to play your part more effectively?

199
We never miss the water until the well runs dry

We take things for granted until they are not available to us.

There may be people contributing to our organisation who do tasks that are not at the forefront of our mind. They ensure that the IT is working, or that invoices are paid and that the website is kept up to date. We seek to remember to acknowledge and affirm their contributions. We recognise the risk that we complain when these services are not available and ignore them when they are working well. We remind ourselves to send notes of thanks to unsung heroes on a regular basis

Rashid would get irritated when the IT was not working effectively. He could be the first to send off an e-mail identifying problems and setting expectations about solutions. He recognised that as a leader he ought to be thinking through what more he could do to enable people who kept the organisation running to do their jobs increasingly effectively. They needed to be listened to and appreciated and not taken for granted.

Reflections
- Who most needs your affirmation and encouragement in areas which do not have a high profile?
- How best do you recognise the contribution of people who keep an enterprise going?
- How best do you anticipate when there could be a breakdown in the infrastructure that supports the enterprise?

Where there is a will there is a way

When there is a clear desire to move forward a solution is normally found.

What is central to any enterprise's success is a passion to make a difference. When there is a rooted set of beliefs in an enterprise and a strong level of commitment and motivation to move forward, the most insurmountable of obstacles can be overcome. It can be valuable for a team to consider 'how strong is our underlying commitment to find a way forward?' Where there is ambivalence, some hard thinking is needed.

Rashid, when faced with a degree of apathy or exhaustion, wanted to give a rousing speech about the way forward. There were times when this was the right step to take, but often what was needed was the exploration with his team about what would enable them to be more energized and committed going forward, and what were some of the blockages. He knew he needed to find a shared motivation and joint will to move forward together in addressing and finding solutions.

Reflections
- When do you need to push forward irrespective of the sceptics around you?
- How best do you build a shared level of commitment to find a solution?
- When do you set out a very clear prospectus yourself and when do you focus on building a strong consensus?

Acknowledgements

I am grateful for the forbearance of my coaching clients when I have suggested metaphors as a means of exploring dilemmas that they are facing. Frequently a metaphor has caught the imagination and allowed a conversation to flow which has explored different aspects of a challenging situation. Following a coaching conversation, it is often the metaphor that has stayed with a coachee allowing them to keep thinking through next steps which we began to discuss in a coaching context.

I want to acknowledge those who have been especially influential in prompting me to think through the relevance of metaphors in leading well. These include Julie Taylor, Ruth Sinclair, Shaun McNally, Sunil Patel, Duncan Selbie, Shirley Rogers, Katie Gardiner, Brian Pomering, Fran Oram, Sophie Langdale, Alex Lambert, and Charlie Massey.

As a youngster I remember an Aunt taking me through lists of metaphors in the book, 'First Aid in English' which helped develop in me a delight in the visual representation of metaphors. Holding onto a metaphor has always been a helpful way for me in keeping up my personal resolve. During tough times in my first career in Government, I trained myself to look for the 'silver lining' in any difficult situation and to remember that there will be 'light at the end of the tunnel', eventually.

My thanks go to colleagues at Praesta Partners who have been sources of practical ideas and have always been willing to challenge my thinking. In particular I want to thank Hilary Douglas, Paul Gray, Louise Shepherd, Janet Rubin and Una O'Brien for their sound advice and perspective.

I am grateful to Lord John Thomas for writing the foreword to the book. John always brings energy and clarity to the issues he is dealing with. He has been an inspiration to me in conversations about how to bring effective leadership when there are conflicting apirations.

Melvin Neo at Marshall Cavendish has been an excellent sponsor for the seven-book series of '100 Great Ideas' and for this book on two hundred metaphors. Janine Gamilla at Marshall Cavendish has provided lots of practical support.

Jackie Tookey has typed the manuscript with her wonderful care and efficiency. Tracy Easthope has managed my diary to enable me to have the space to write. Together, Jackie and Tracy have been an excellent support team to whom I owe a great deal. Anthony Hopkins and Jo Gavin have provided valuable support in enabling me to do my coaching work at Praesta Partners.

I am grateful to Zoe Stear who has read the manuscript in detail and given me constructive feedback enabling me to bring greater clarity in the way some of the metaphors have been elucidated.

My family have been consistently supportive of the coaching and writing and are always ready to tease me when I appear to go into coaching mode. I am indebted to them and my grandchildren for bringing a sense of fun. It has been a delight to dedicate the book to our grandchildren who are a delight to Frances and me.

Books and booklets by Peter Shaw

Mirroring Jesus as Leader. Cambridge: Grove, 2004

Conversation Matters: how to engage effectively with one another. London: Continuum, 2005

The Four Vs of Leadership: vision, values, value-added, and vitality. Chichester: Capstone, 2006

Finding Your Future: the second time around. London: Darton, Longman and Todd, 2006

Business Coaching: achieving practical results through effective engagement. Chichester: Capstone, 2007 (co-authored with Robin Linnecar)

Making Difficult Decisions: how to be decisive and get the business done. Chichester: Capstone, 2008

Deciding Well: a Christian perspective on making decisions as a leader. Vancouver: Regent College Publishing, 2009

Raise Your Game: how to succeed at work. Chichester: Capstone, 2009

Effective Christian Leaders in the Global Workplace. Colorado Springs: Authentic/Paternoster, 2010

Defining Moments: navigating through business and organisational life. Basingstoke: Palgrave/Macmillan, 2010

The Reflective Leader: standing still to move forward. Norwich: Canterbury Press, 2011 (co-authored with Alan Smith)

Thriving in Your Work: how to be motivated and do well in challenging times. London: Marshall Cavendish, 2011

Getting the Balance Right: leading and managing well. London: Marshall Cavendish, 2013

Leading in Demanding Times. Cambridge: Grove, 2013 (co-authored with Graham Shaw)

The Emerging Leader: stepping up in leadership. Norwich: Canterbury Press, 2013, (co-authored with Colin Shaw)

100 Great Personal Impact Ideas. London: Marshall Cavendish, 2013

100 Great Coaching Ideas. London: Marshall Cavendish 2014

Celebrating Your Senses. Delhi: ISPCK, 2014

Sustaining Leadership: renewing your strength and sparkle. Norwich: Canterbury Press, 2014

100 Great Team Effectiveness Ideas. London: Marshall Cavendish, 2015

Wake Up and Dream: stepping into your future. Norwich: Canterbury Press, 2015

100 Great Building Success Ideas. London: Marshall Cavendish, 2016

The Reluctant Leader: coming out of the shadows. Norwich: Canterbury Press, 2016 (co-authored with Hilary Douglas)

100 Great Leading Well Ideas. London: Marshall Cavendish, 2016

Living with never-ending expectations. Vancouver: Regent College Publishing 2017 (co-authored with Graham Shaw)

100 Great Handling Rapid Change Ideas. London: Marshall Cavendish, 2018

The Mindful Leader: embodying Christian principles. Norwich: Canterbury Press, 2018

100 Great Leading Through Frustration Ideas. London: Marshall Cavendish, 2019

Leadership to the Limits: freedom and responsibility. Norwich: Canterbury Press, 2020

The Power of Leadership Metaphors, London: Marshall Cavendish, 2021

Forthcoming

Those Blessed Leaders. Vancouver: Regent College Publishing, 2021

Shaping your Future, Norwich: Canterbury Press, 2022

Booklets

Riding the Rapids. London: Praesta, 2008 (co-authored with Jane Stephens)

Seizing the Future. London: Praesta, 2010 (co-authored with Robin Hindle-Fisher)

Living Leadership: finding equilibrium, London: Praesta, 2011

The Age of Agility. London: Praesta, 2012 (co-authored with Steve Wigzell)

Knowing the Score: what we can learn from music and musicians. London: Praesta, 2016 (co-authored with Ken Thompson)

The Resilient Team. London: Praesta 2017 (co-authored with Hilary Douglas)

Job Sharing: a model for the future workplace. London: Praesta 2018 (co-authored with Hilary Douglas)

The Four Vs of Leadership: vision, values, value-added and vitality. London: Praesta 2019

The Resilient Leader. London: Praesta 2020 (co-authored with Hilary Douglas)

Leading for the Long Term: creating a sustainable future. London: Praesta 2021 (co-authored with Hilary Douglas)

(Copies of the booklets above can be downloaded from the Praesta website)

About the Author

Peter Shaw has coached individuals, senior teams and groups across six continents. He is a Visiting Professor of Leadership Development at Chester, De Montfort, Newcastle, Huddersfield, and Surrey Universities, and is a Professorial Fellow at St John's College, Durham University. He has been a member of the Visiting Professorial Faculty at Regent College, Vancouver since 2008 and is a Visiting Professor at the Judicial College in Melbourne. He has written 30 books on aspects of leadership: some have been translated into seven different languages.

Peter's first career was in the UK Government where he worked in five Government Departments and held three Director General posts. Peter has been a member of governing bodies in higher and further education. He is a licensed lay minister (Reader) in the Anglican Church and plays an active role in the Church of England at parish, diocesan and national levels. He is a Lay Canon of Guildford Cathedral and Chair of Guildford Cathedral Council.

Peter holds a doctorate in Leadership Development from Chester University. He was awarded an honorary doctorate at Durham University for 'outstanding service to public life', and an honorary doctorate by Huddersfield University for his contribution to leadership and management.

In his coaching work Peter enables leaders and teams to use their freedoms as leaders to best effect. Peter draws from his wide experience both as a leader and as a coach to leaders in many different contexts. He seeks to bring insights drawn from his wealth of experience and underpinned by his Christian faith and understanding. His focus is on enabling individuals and teams to step up in their effectiveness so that they have a clear vision about what they are seeking to do, apply the values that are most important to them, know how to bring a distinctive value-added and recognise their sources of vitality.

Peter has completed forty long-distance walks in the UK, with the Yorkshire Dales being his most favoured area for walking. Seven grandchildren help him belie the fact that he was born in the first half of the 20th Century.

INDEX OF METAPHORS

NB: Numbers listed are as per the sequence and not the page number where the metaphor is explained

The light at the end of the tunnel 3
The next mountain to climb 7
The puzzled shrug of the shoulders 184
The road not taken 176
The rocks in the way 4
The seed has to die 1
The wheel has come full circle 171
There has to be an ending before there can be a new beginning 5
There is no virtue like necessity 172
Three steps forward and two steps back 58
Three strikes and you are out 90
Throw in the sponge too early 150
Time to blaze a trail 10
Too many cooks spoil the broth 78
Truth has many dimensions 46
Truth will out 45
Turkeys don't vote for Christmas 192
Turn over a new leaf 101
Turn the tables 9
Turn up your nose 125
Two heads are better than one 77

Use the long screwdriver occasionally 87

Wait till the clouds roll by 64
Walk before you run 95
Watch dwelling on broken dreams 181
Watch getting caught in the vortex 180
Watch getting steamed up 47
Watch if familiarity breeds contempt 52
Watch if your heart is in your boots 114
Watch the chip on the shoulder 113
We have two ears and one mouth 37
We never miss the water until the well runs dry 199
What goes up comes down 97
When one door closes another opens 2
Where there is a will there is a way 200
Withdraw gracefully 187

You can't make a silk purse out of a sow's ear 53